THE DARK TOWER

THE
DARK TOWER

A
MELODRAMA

by

Alexander Woollcott

and

George S. Kaufman

RANDOM HOUSE · NEW YORK · 1934

PRINTED IN THE UNITED STATES OF AMERICA
BY VAN REES PRESS, NEW YORK CITY

14015

"The Dark Tower" was produced by Sam H. Harris at the Morosco Theatre, New York City, on Saturday night, November 25th, 1933, with the following cast:

HATTIE	Margaret Hamilton
MARTHA TEMPLE	Margaret Dale
BEN WESTON	William Harrigan
DAMON WELLS	Basil Sidney
DAPHNE MARTIN	Leona Maricle
JESSICA WELLS	Margalo Gillmore
BARRY JONES	John Griggs
DR. KENDALL	John T. Doyle
STANLEY VANCE	Ernest Milton
A TAXI DRIVER	Charles Romano
MAX SARNOFF	Anton Stengel
PATSY DOWLING	Beatrice Blinn
A BELLBOY	William MacFadden
WILLIAM CURTIS	Porter Hall

SCENES

Act I.

A House in East 48th St., New York City. Saturday Night.

Act II.

Scene 1. The House. A Week Later.
Scene 2. A Room in the Waldorf-Astoria.

Act III.

Scene 1. The House Again. Five Days Later.
Scene 2. The House. The Next Day.

ACT ONE

ACT ONE

*The scene is the ground-floor living-room of a house in the
East Forties, New York City.*

*The time is the present. It is midnight on a Saturday in late
September. At one side a great double doorway, hung with
looped curtains of lemon-colored velvet, leads into the hall.
Opposite, double doors give upon the adjoining room. Tucked
away under the staircase a small swinging door communicates
with the pantry.*

*This staircase is a tremendous affair leading with a flourish
to the floor above. At its first turn there is a railed landing from
which a candidate for public office could effectively receive the
deputation notifying him of his nomination. A piano stands at
a bay window. The window-panes are of colored glass to shield
the room from the gaze of passers-by.*

*All the furniture is of the late eighties, heavy and shabby.
The room appears to have been decorated by a process of ac-
cumulation. The most conspicuous item is a portrait which
hangs at the foot of the stairs, beside an ornate wall-clock. This
portrait reveals a Cardinal of the Church of Rome with his
hand uplifted in what appears to be malediction. It may be
guessed that his were the Cardinal's hat and mittens which are
carefully preserved under a glass case on the mantel-piece, between the two tall lamps with their fringes of green crystal.*

*At first glance this would seem to be the home of a some-
what flamboyant prelate, which makes more puzzling the fact
that at the rising of the curtain two elderly women are discovered*

II

engaged in a game of cribbage. These are MISS MARTHA TEMPLE, *a handsome and acrid woman of sixty whose house this is, and* HATTIE, *who has been her maidservant for more than thirty years.* HATTIE *is dressed in vintage alpaca with a white apron.* MISS TEMPLE *makes all her plays swiftly and has long suffered from* HATTIE's *indecision, which is emphasized by her obnoxious habit of supplying each game with incidental music in the form of "The Shade of the Old Apple Tree," sung softly as she plays, with no great attention to the words.*

HATTIE

Your cut. (MISS TEMPLE *rises formally, goes round her chair once, resumes her seat, places her hand on the deck, lifts her eyes to Heaven in silent prayer, cuts the cards, and* HATTIE *turns up a jack*) Two for his nobs. (*She takes the two points while* MISS TEMPLE, *still looking upward, reveals by her expression her displeasure with the Almighty.*)

MISS TEMPLE

Ten.

HATTIE

Fifteen. (*Scoring it.*)

MISS TEMPLE

Twenty-five.

HATTIE

Thirty-one. (*Scoring it.*)

MISS TEMPLE

Four.

HATTIE

And a pair is eight.

12

MISS TEMPLE

And one is nine.

HATTIE

Fourteen. Last card. One for me.

MISS TEMPLE
(*With immense sarcasm*)
Only one. Too bad. (*Counting her hand*) Fifteen two, fifteen four, fifteen six. (*The doorbell rings*) Who's that?

HATTIE
(*Rising*)
Fifteen two, four, six and a pair is eight and a run of three is eleven. (*She pegs this, and, snatching up her crib, starts for the door, counting as she goes*) Double run of four--that makes ten for Hattie. (*She has reached the door.*)

MISS TEMPLE
(*As* HATTIE *vanishes into the hallway*)
I want to see it.

WESTON
(*His voice heard in the hall*)
Is Miss Wells here yet?

HATTIE

No, she isn't.

MISS TEMPLE

Who's that?

WESTON
(*As he enters*)
Oh, I'm sorry. I'm Ben Weston.

(WESTON *is a tall, graying man in his late forties, with a deep, friendly voice. There is nothing of the theatrical manager about him. He is a theatrical manager.*)

MISS TEMPLE

(*As* HATTIE *takes the visitor's hat*)

Oh, yes, Mr. Weston. I'm Miss Temple, Jessica's aunt. She ought to be here soon now. The doctor went out to Greenwich to get her. (*To* HATTIE, *who is prudently advancing her peg,* WESTON's *hat still in her free hand*) What are you doing, Hattie?

HATTIE

My crib. Ten.

MISS TEMPLE

(*Glancing at the hand and acknowledging it with a grudging grunt, then gathering all the cards to shuffle and deal*)

You won't mind if we just finish this game? It won't take long, I'm afraid.

HATTIE

I've got her almost skunked. (*She hands* WESTON's *hat back to him abstractedly, resumes her seat and gathers up the six cards dealt her.*)

WESTON

What is this, euchre or something?

MISS TEMPLE

Cribbage.

WESTON

Cribbage? I thought only sea-captains played that.

HATTIE

Live and learn. (HATTIE *is once more in the throes of lyric discard—"In the Shade of the Old Apple Tree."*)

MISS TEMPLE
(*Watching her with smoldering rage*)
You don't happen to be putting on a comic opera this season, do you, Mr. Weston? Hattie's been working on that number for twenty-nine years. Of course she doesn't know many of the words yet.

WESTON
Just not a quick study.

MISS TEMPLE
(*As* HATTIE, *thus goaded, parts defiantly with two cards, and cuts the deck*)
Of course, *I* wouldn't get a jack.

HATTIE
(*Leading a card*)
Ten.

MISS TEMPLE
Eleven.

HATTIE
Fifteen. (*She scores the two points.*)

MISS TEMPLE
Twenty-five.

HATTIE
Thirty-one. I'm out.

MISS TEMPLE
And I'm skunked. Get my Ovaltine. (MISS TEMPLE *sweeps up the cards, puts them in the drawer of the cribbage board, totals up the game score, and from the cribbage board extracts the score royal, on which she records* HATTIE's *triumph*) Four-

15

twenty-three on the week. I'll never catch up with her. She's sold her soul to the devil.

(HATTIE, *passing through the pantry door at this moment, flirts her behind gayly as she exits.*)

WESTON

Do you play for money?

MISS TEMPLE

Worse than that. The loser cleans the silverware. (WESTON *gives a cluck of sympathy. She holds out her nails for him to see*) There's the score for you. She hasn't touched the polish since the second week in May.

WESTON

What does she do while you polish? Sit and watch?

MISS TEMPLE

(*Taking up her knitting and starting to work*)
Goes to the movies. So if you want to see her Monday afternoon, drop in at Loew's Lexington.

WESTON

I'll be there. (*Glancing from his watch to the clock on the wall*) Your clock right?

MISS TEMPLE

Wouldn't think so.

WESTON

I've got ten after twelve. Sorry to break in on you at such an hour, but I've got some business with those young people of yours.

MISS TEMPLE

(*Knitting away throughout*)
They'll be here any minute. And the Lord knows who else.

16

WESTON

How is Jessica? Standing up under it?

MISS TEMPLE

Thriving. Still a little shaky, but better every day.

WESTON

I knew that's all she needed. Once back in the theatre, she'd be herself again.

MISS TEMPLE

Well, I hope you're right. Let me tell you this, Mr. Weston—there's been a miracle. I've lived with her through this thing, and I never thought she'd act again.

WESTON

It's been three years, hasn't it?

MISS TEMPLE

Three years last February. It was a Tuesday night.

WESTON
(*With a sigh*)

Yes, I know. (*She looks at him*) You see—I was there.

MISS TEMPLE

That night?

WESTON
(*Nods*)

I saw her drop. I was there when they dismissed the audience.

MISS TEMPLE

I aged ten years that night.

WESTON

You weren't at the theatre?

17

MISS TEMPLE

(*Shakes her head*)

They telephoned up about ten-thirty—company manager. Hattie took the message and was useless from then on. Damon was in Hollywood. I stood out on the stoop and waited till the ambulance came. They had her on a stretcher. She didn't know me or anybody. It was six months before she said a word.

WESTON

It must have been ghastly for you.

MISS TEMPLE

It was her apathy that broke your heart. She didn't care whether she lived or died. You'd have thought she'd been drugged. I suppose every one said it *was* drugs, didn't they?

WESTON

There were all kinds of stories.

MISS TEMPLE

There would be. But the truth was worse than any of them.

WESTON

(*A pause*)

I've been kind of hoping, these last three months, that some one would tell me just what the truth was.

MISS TEMPLE

I was always for telling it.

WESTON

Well?

MISS TEMPLE

It was that husband of hers. Did you ever know the Honorable Stanley Vance?

18

WESTON

I met him once.

MISS TEMPLE

He was the lowest form of animal life.

WESTON

Dead, isn't he?

MISS TEMPLE

Yes, God be praised. Otherwise she'd never be acting out in Greenwich this week.

WESTON

I don't quite understand. Do you mean he kept her from acting? What did he do to her?

MISS TEMPLE

Ever see a snake with a bird, Mr. Weston? Well, that was Jessica and Stanley Vance. Of course, when she stopped earning money, we never saw him again. Then one day we got the good news. Some anonymous benefactor, doing a little target practice on a San Francisco street-corner, had put an abrupt end to the earthly career of my dear nephew-in-law. Hit him in the stomach, I believe. I was so pleased.

WESTON

The spell had been broken.

MISS TEMPLE

The devil had been cast out. Stanley Vance with a bullet in his stomach—that was all the medicine she needed.

WESTON

(Shoving his hands in his pockets, walking to the window and then coming back)

19

I'm glad you told me that, Miss Temple. It's a horrifying story, but in a way it's a kind of relief. A relief to know she's not just one of those who have the jitters about nothing at all. When I found this play and took it to Damon, it was because I couldn't imagine any one in the world but Jessica playing it. Mind you, if I knew she could play it only two weeks, I'd still take her. If only for the thrill of coming out of the Astor each night and seeing that sign in lights over my theatre—"Jessica Wells in 'The Dark Tower.'"

MISS TEMPLE

How about "Ben Weston Presents"?

WESTON

Well, that too. And what you've just told me kind of makes me think that sign might be there for a year. I could stand a little success. And what a relief it will be to have a show in that theatre I can look at myself without getting sick at my stomach. And what an actress! In her last show, I used to drop in almost every night around ten and stand up at the back and catch that scene of hers in the second act. That's how I happened to be there when— (*An eloquent gesture*) She's a great actress, all right—a great actress.

MISS TEMPLE

She's all right if you like acting.

WESTON

Yes, and Damon's a great actor.

MISS TEMPLE

If you can call a man an actor who doesn't act. He's a great drinker.

20

WESTON

Funny thing, too. Their father, if I may say so, was terrible. No offense.

MISS TEMPLE

None whatever. You put it mildly. (*Gesturing toward the portrait above the piano*) Lionel Wells as Cardinal Richelieu. Pronouncing the curse of Rome, at a dollar top.

WESTON

(*Looking around*)

Say, I've been in this room before. God, it must have been twenty-five years ago. I was working for Charley Frohman. The room was different. Those stairs weren't there.

MISS TEMPLE

He had them put in the year before he died. Used that landing for making entrances. Once he made a dreadful mistake. Came on when nobody was looking.

WESTON

Say! He was in a nasty jam.

MISS TEMPLE

Oh, no. He had great presence of mind. Went back and came on again.

WESTON

Yes, I remember the whole thing now. Frohman had offered him a part, but I guess it couldn't have been a very good one. Anyhow, I was sent up for the script, and I got it—from a distance of about twenty feet. He may not have been much of an actor, Miss Temple, but he'd have made a great outfielder. Was he any good as a father?

21

MISS TEMPLE

Oh, he gave a pretty good performance as a father. Never had to sustain the character for any long stretch. When the children were little, he was generally away.

WESTON

I know. The eternal road star. He thought the syndicate kept him out of New York.

MISS TEMPLE

Wish they'd kept him out of Albany. If they had I'd still be there.

WESTON

Don't tell me you ran away with him.

MISS TEMPLE

No, but my sister did. My fault, too. It was my idea to go to that matinée—Lionel Wells in "The Prisoner of Zenda." The curtain hadn't been up five minutes before the damage was done. My life was a wreck. (*As* HATTIE *enters with a tray, pot and cup*) Have some Ovaltine, Mr. Weston?

WESTON

No, thanks, I'm off the stuff. Albany, eh? Harmanus Bleecker Hall.

HATTIE

You from Albany?

WESTON

God, no. But I was ahead of "Ben Hur" for three seasons. That's the way to see America.

HATTIE

I came from Kinderhook. That's not far from Albany.

22

WESTON
(*Graciously*)

Well!

HATTIE

Martin Van Buren came from there, too.

WESTON

That's fine. (*To* MISS TEMPLE) Whatever made you come to New York to live?

MISS TEMPLE

I didn't come to New York to live. I came down for two weeks to take care of Janie. It was when she was going to have Jessica. You think Jessica's pretty, don't you, Mr. Weston?

WESTON

I think she's lovely.

MISS TEMPLE
(*With a grunt*)

You should have seen Janie. She died, Mr. Weston. She died having Jessica. So I stayed on for a while to look after things. (*She gives a snort*) Of course, later I sent for my trunks and Hattie and subscribed to the *Knickerbocker Press*. That was in the Fall of 1901—the year they shot McKinley. I'm still here. Yes, sir, still here. (*To* HATTIE) Did you get some Liederkranz for Mr. Damon?

HATTIE

Of course.

MISS TEMPLE

Plenty of beer in the icebox?

HATTIE

Four bottles.

MISS TEMPLE

Better put some more on. You can't tell how long they'll sit and guzzle. We're back on the stage, Hattie. (HATTIE *goes out*) Damon said some of you might come in for supper. I was brought up to think supper was something you ate at six o'clock—cold meat and chow-chow and cinnamon cake. If I live another twenty years, they'll be having supper for breakfast.

WESTON

And it all began with "The Prisoner of Zenda."

MISS TEMPLE

Yes, sir, I often think of that matinée. We hadn't meant to go at all. We were late and dropped in on a chance. Janie stopped to look at the photographs in the lobby—while I went up to the box office and asked if they had two seats. I wonder where we'd all be now if the man had said no.

> (*There's a sound of the outer door opening.* DAMON WELLS *comes in with a rush, preceded by the sound of his voice and followed by* DAPHNE MARTIN, *a tall, dark, sullen beauty of twenty, wearing a dress of great chic and an air of permanent resentment.* DAMON *is thirty-seven, sloppy in an unpressed suit, slouchy in gait.*)

DAMON

Bottle of beer, Liederkranz, and plenty of— (*He enters*) Good God, the management!

WESTON

Sir Henry Irving, I presume?

DAMON

What are you doing here? (*Yelling*) Hattie!

24

MISS TEMPLE

I'll get it for you. Where's Jessica?

DAMON

Driving in with the Doc. I took the train.

DAPHNE

We took the train.

DAMON

Bless me, so we did. I'd forgotten this little kitten. Aunt Martha—Miss Daphne Martin, America's most wooden actress.

MISS TEMPLE

How do you do, my dear? I saw you in the play. I thought you were excellent.

DAPHNE

It's a lousy part.

DAMON

(With malignant gentleness)

Wait till you see an actress in it, my dear.

MISS TEMPLE

You know, I kept thinking I'd seen you before.

DAPHNE

Lucky Strikes.

MISS TEMPLE
(Puzzled)

Lucky Strikes?

DAMON

She poses for them. She's posing now. Get her a Scotch and soda. (*He passes his hat to* DAPHNE) Here, my winsome creature.

25

(MISS TEMPLE *goes*.) You should have seen us to-night, Ben. Pretty good show.

WESTON

Good house?

DAMON

Best yet. Saturday night, of course. (*To* DAPHNE, *who stands holding his hat*) Put it down somewhere. (*She places it with elaborate care on the telephone-stand*) Hattie! (*To* WESTON) But the second act needs fixing. Say, why weren't you out there to-night? Jessica said you were coming out.

WESTON

Well, that brings me to my story.

DAMON

(*Starting for the dining-room*)

Be right with you. (*As he disappears*) Hattie, for God's sake!

DAPHNE

(*Half-aloud*)

The son-of-a— (*She forms the word with her lips.*)

WESTON

I beg your pardon. I didn't catch the end of that.

DAPHNE

I'll give you three guesses.

WESTON

So that's the way you feel about him.

DAPHNE

Well, it gives you a rough idea.

WESTON

What's your complaint?

26

DAPHNE

Forgets he's out with me half the time. Leaves me sticking in umbrella stands.

WESTON

Why do you stand for it? Why don't you walk out on him?

DAPHNE

I can't.

WESTON

Why can't you?

DAPHNE

Be no fun in it. He doesn't want me enough.

DAMON

(*Reappearing with a napkin stuck in his collar, a plate in one hand, a beer-mug in the other*)

All right, what's on your mind? Listen, my trailing arbutus, go right through there and mix yourself a hell of a drink and stay till I ring for you. You can be thinking about your art. (*She starts slowly towards the dining-room, throwing* WESTON *a meaningful glance*) Scamper, scamper! (*He advances to the table*) Say, don't you want something to eat?

WESTON

No, Lord Chesterfield, I don't. Listen, Damon, the show's pretty good, eh?

DAMON

(*With his mouth full*)

Looked good to-night.

WESTON

Then—look here! Why do we have to wait four or five weeks? Why can't it come right in?

27

DAMON

What do you mean, right in?

WESTON

Week from Monday. Labor Day night.

DAMON

You mean your theatre?

WESTON

Exactly.

DAMON

But you've got a show in there.

WESTON

(*Shakes his head*)

Not since 11:15 to-night.

DAMON

But it only opened Wednesday.

WESTON

It's not there now.

DAMON

Must have been a little gem.

WESTON

It was. All about puberty. And when I say all about puberty I mean ALL about puberty. Everybody in it was just discovering sex, and with considerable surprise. The trouble was, it was no news to the audience.

DAMON

Yes, I guess there's enough sex in real life without going to the theatre for it.

28

WESTON

And the cast, Damon. I told them that sixty-year-old character actor was just a bit mature for the part of the schoolboy.
(*He sighs deeply*) So here I am with a dark theatre on my
hands.

DAMON

(*Taking a long draught from his mug*)
Good God! Come in a week from Monday!

WESTON

Why not? Your show's a hit. What are we waiting for?
Jessica could come in to-morrow. It's going to be a triumph
for that little sister of yours.

DAMON

Now hold on a minute. Of course *she'll* be great in it. But
there's a lot to be done yet. That second act.

WESTON

One little scene. A couple of hours' work.

DAMON

My part. Who's going to play *my* part?

WESTON

Well, we'll have to get some one. We'd have to do that anyway.

DAMON

But in a week. Where you going to find him? Actors' Dinner
Club?

WESTON

Of course we probably won't get as good a performance as
you gave.

29

DAMON

What do you mean "probably"?

WESTON

Still won't play it yourself, huh? Won't consider it?

DAMON

Not for a minute. I don't want to act. You know that. I promised myself five years ago I'd never act again.

WESTON

You acted in Greenwich. You acted all over the stage.

DAMON

I don't count Greenwich.

WESTON

Now listen here. For three seasons you were the best God-damned actor in America. There was no argument.

DAMON

I hate argument.

WESTON

Then you quit cold. Where've you been since? On your pratt in Hollywood. Drunk half the time and the other half directing Lionel Atwell.

DAMON

I can't be drunk *all* the time.

WESTON

What beats me is why any one with a talent like yours should bury it in a napkin. You belong on the stage.

DAMON

But I hate acting. Do you know what my trouble is? I can't

fake. I have to strip myself at every performance. Christ, I hate giving up my guts for the entertainment of every passerby who happens to have fifty cents. A trained bear with a ring in his nose. No, thank you, Mr. Weston.

WESTON

I get you. You don't want to do it.

DAMON

There's no keeping anything from you.

WESTON

Well, no harm in having tried once more. I sort of hoped you might do it for Jessica's sake.

DAMON

That's not fair, Ben. I dropped everything out there the moment her tide turned. You can't guess what those weeks meant, when we were getting her courage back. Day by day, a step at a time. So slow. So anxious. Then this show. I even went on the wagon for it. I directed it the best I could and didn't take a nickel for it. I even put paint on my cheeks and strutted around the suburbs. It isn't as if the play depended on my acting in it. After all, it's the woman's play. Any fair actor can do my part. Leslie Howard, Alfred Lunt. It doesn't need me. No, Ben, I'll see you through to the New York opening and then I'm washed up.

WESTON

What'll you do then?

DAMON

I don't know. (*A happy thought strikes him*) May get drunk permanently. (*Yelling*) Hattie!

31

WESTON

(*Rising*)

By the way, Damon, I don't know whether you meant me to know it, but before you got here, the old lady told me a little something about that fellow Vance.

DAMON

(*Somberly*)

Did she? Well, whatever she told you was the truth.

WESTON

I've been puzzling about it ever since she told me.

DAMON

I've been puzzling about it ever since it happened.

WESTON

Well, at least it settles one thing. It proves once and for all that Jessica is a great actress.

DAMON

How's it do that?

WESTON

The fact that she married a guy like that. Did you ever meet the husbands of our best actresses? Whew! What a collection!

DAMON

(*musingly*)

Say, that's right! There's— (*He decides not to name names*) That's right.

WESTON

I met Vance once. Ratty sort. What did he have—some kind of power over her?

32

DAMON

Some unholy fascination, I suppose. They say he could make her do anything. I didn't see much of it. When she first brought him home I took a dislike to him, and—simply got out. Rotten thing to have done, I suppose, but could I guess how it was going to turn out?

WESTON

(*After a struggle*)

Was she—in love with him?

DAMON

It started out that way, I suppose. Later on—

HATTIE

(*Entering with fresh beer and cheese*)

Want some more beer?

DAMON

Huh? (*Turning*) Well, if it isn't the Serpent of Old Nile. Hattie, you grow more voluptuous every week.

HATTIE

(*immensely gratified*)

That girl out in the kitchen—she's just sitting there.

DAMON

What girl?

HATTIE

Didn't she come in with you?

DAMON

Oh, yes. Is she still here?

HATTIE

She's awful cross. What's she mad about?

33

DAMON

Mad about me, Hattie. You should be the last to blame her.

MISS TEMPLE

(*Entering from the dining-room*)
Damon, you're not being very polite to Miss Martin.

DAMON

Not polite! Me? I resent that. And Hattie resents it. Don't you, Hattie? You're furious, aren't you? Aunt Martha, you've grossly offended Hattie, who has been with us for many years, and who, if she has an ounce of pride, will walk out of this house this minute.

DAPHNE

(*Appearing in the doorway with a highball in her hand*)
I'm going home.

DAMON

There you are! Another one! They're all leaving! Quitting like rats! (JESSICA WELLS *enters from the street, followed by* DR. KENDALL *and* BARRY JONES. *She is thirty-two, fair and frail.* DR. KENDALL, *who is sixty, is little, quiet and distinguished.* BARRY JONES *is a faintly collegiate, eager blushing youth of twenty-four.* JESSICA *pauses for a moment on the threshold.* DAMON *swings in her direction and points at her accusingly*)
What are you doing here? How dare you? How dare you set foot inside this house?

JESSICA

How dare I? What have I to lose? What worse thing can you or any one do to me than you have already done?

HATTIE

Miss Jessica!

34

DAMON

Than *I* have done? That's good! That's rich, that is! Was it I who made our name a rotten joke in this town? Was it I who fouled this nest? Was it I who stole out of here in the middle of the night—

JESSICA

Stop! That's all over and done with. I sat in that court to-day and heard a little old man in a black robe announce that I was not fit to have charge of my own child. That was your mistake.

DAMON

What can you do about it?

JESSICA

You little guess how much I can do about it. I'm going to fight you with weapons which only one short day ago I would have scorned to touch. I did not live three hideous years under this roof without learning certain things about you and your precious family. I know your secret—the secret you would all rather die than hear told. And I'm going to tell it. I'm going to shout it in the streets! I'm going to make your name a by-word in this town! I'm going to pull your house down over your head, so help me God!

DAMON

God damn it, no! Why do you always break down there? You did that to-night. You're not sorry for yourself. You're mad! You're furious! Save your quavers—you're going to need them.

JESSICA

(*Holding his face in her hands*)

I know. I know. You're perfectly right. I did, didn't I? It's sickening. Now let me try it again. (*She slaps him fondly and goes back a few steps*) Give me the cue.

DAMON

(*In a dead voice*)
What can you do about it?

JESSICA

How can I get mad at that?

DAMON and BARRY

(*In unison,* DAMON *speaking with tremendous intensity*)
What can you do about it?

JESSICA

(*Mumbling*)
You little guess how much I can do about it ... fight you ... weapons ... scorn to touch ... hideous years ... (*At full tilt, with* BARRY, *in his eagerness, saying the same words inaudibly*) I know your secret ... the secret you would all rather die than hear told. And I'm going to tell it! I'm going to shout it in the streets! I'm going to make your name a byword in this town!

DAMON

Now let's have it!

JESSICA

I'm going to pull your house down over your heads, so help me God!

DAMON

That's the stuff!

JESSICA

(*Suddenly stricken by the sight of* HATTIE. *Speaks in a hushed tone*)
Arthur, we've waked him. My darling, you shouldn't have

36

come downstairs at such an hour. (*She goes to* HATTIE *and tenderly embraces her.*)

HATTIE

Huh?

JESSICA

Why did you get up, my sweet? Didn't Nursie tuck you in all comfy? (*Abruptly handing* HATTIE *her coat*) Hattie, I'm famished. You know what I want. Tea and a great big bowl of salad. Barry, dear, want anything to eat? Doctor? Hattie, what's in the icebox? Aunt Martha, this is Barry Jones. He wrote the play. Wasn't it sweet of him? Ben, dear, I could have wept when you didn't come out to-night. Now, why did you fail me? (*She sinks into the chair at the left of the table, tosses her hat on the sofa, runs her fingers through her hair.*)

WESTON

I was trapped like a rat.

DR. KENDALL

(*To* MISS TEMPLE *as he starts for the dining-room*) Martha, may I prowl?

MISS TEMPLE

Same old lemon-juice?

HATTIE

(*En route to the kitchen*)
It's in the icebox. (*The* DOCTOR *goes out.*)

DAMON

(*Who has sat down on the couch, clutching at her apron as she passes*)

Hattie!

HATTIE

Huh?

DAMON

(*In a stage whisper*)

Come to my room later!

(*She flounces out, vastly delighted.*)

JESSICA

Barry, where are you? Tell Aunt Martha what you want to eat, and you might as well start currying favor with her right now. If she doesn't like you we shan't be allowed to do any more of your lovely plays. Sorry!

BARRY

How does one curry favor with you, Miss Temple?

MISS TEMPLE

Oh, just an occasional chuck under the chin.

DAMON

(*Who has now settled, as for the night, on the couch*)

She likes emeralds, too.

MISS TEMPLE

(*Who has gathered up the débris of* DAMON'S *supper*)

You look pretty young to me, Mr. Jones, to be a playwright.

BARRY

Young? I'm twenty-four. Noel Coward was only twenty-three when he wrote "The Vortex."

DAMON

Noel Coward was twenty-three for five consecutive seasons.

BARRY

And when Sheldon wrote "Salvation Nell," he was only twenty-two.

38

DAMON

And Chatterton was only eighteen when he hanged himself.

MISS TEMPLE

(*As she starts for the dining-room*)
Well, you growing boys need nourishment. I'll see what I can scare up. (*She goes out.*)

BARRY

Wish you'd been out there to-night, B.W. We had three standees.

WESTON

You one of them?

BARRY

No, I mean three others. The house-manager says we did the best business they've done there this Summer. That's a good sign, isn't it?

WESTON

Well, did they have any other shows there this Summer?

JESSICA

Don't tease him, Ben.

DAMON

Of course the acid-test, Barry, will come when we play in a town that isn't full of your relatives. That's the reason we turned down O'Neill's play. He's an orphan. (*Hauling himself up to a sitting posture*) And that reminds me, how did they come to christen you Barry? Barry! They didn't know then you were going to be a playwright.

BARRY

Well, Barry's my middle name.

DAMON

Oh, ho! Now it comes out. What's your first name? Sir James?

BARRY

It's Horace.

DAMON

Oh, Horace. Well, it's damned white of you to tell us. Horace B. Jones.

WESTON

I never would have produced the play if I'd known that.
(HATTIE *comes in with* JESSICA's *salad and tea.*)

JESSICA
(*As she draws up her chair*)
I don't care what they say, Barry—

DAMON
(*Interrupting*)
Horace.

JESSICA

I think you're the sweetest playwright I ever had—thank you, Hattie—and I don't ever want to do plays written by anybody else. But I do wish you wouldn't talk quite so much like the latest issue of "Variety."

BARRY

I guess I did sound pretty complacent. I can't help being tickled about the business, but don't think I don't know it's all due to you. Why, (*magnanimously*) I'd rather have you in my play and have it play to empty benches than have anybody else in it and have it a success,

40

DAMON

That was put very nicely.

JESSICA

Perhaps it would be better, Barry, if you didn't talk at all. I tell you what you do. There's a lovely old cracked piano up there and you play divinely. Anyway, I like music with my meals.

BARRY
(*Retreating upstage*)
What'll I play?

JESSICA

Anything, Barry. Something you know, dear. (*As she pours her tea and the music plays for an appreciable interval,* DAPHNE *appears in the doorway*) I like that.

DAPHNE

Who brought the orchestra? Oh, it's you. Play "Stormy Weather." (*She carries her drink to the piano and takes up a posture there.*)

WESTON
(*His hand closing over hers for a second*)
Happy?

JESSICA

Utterly.

WESTON

I'm glad.

JESSICA

But you should have seen me at nine o'clock to-night, when you hadn't shown up. It gave me an incredible sense of misfortune. Ben, I seem to be getting terribly dependent on you.

41

WESTON

That's all the music I need.

JESSICA

And while we're on the subject, where *were* you?

WESTON

Well, that's what I came up here about. It seems I've got a theatre on my hands—

DAPHNE

Play "Stormy Weather."

JESSICA

(*Interrupting as she sees* DR. KENDALL *appear in the doorway*)
Doctor, I love you. Come over here and meet our manager. Ben, this is the oldest friend I have. I couldn't have an older one.

WESTON

(*Rising and shaking hands*)
Doctor, I've seen you at a distance.

KENDALL

I'm told it lends enchantment.

JESSICA

I've known the doctor for thirty-two years, three months and—and—what date is this?

KENDALL

I brought her into the world, Mr. Weston. I keep hoping she won't hold it against me.

JESSICA

There have been times,

42

WESTON

From all I hear, Doctor, you're entitled to a piece of this show.

JESSICA

He didn't think, when that first call came, it was going to be a life job.

KENDALL

Well, it gives me something to do. I'm supposed to be retired, Mr. Weston.

WESTON

Retired? I didn't know doctors ever gave up.

KENDALL

Well, sometimes we lose faith.

JESSICA

How can you say that? Ben, he knows more about medicine than any man in this city.

WESTON

My God, I can't understand you people. I've got a man over on that sofa who knows more about acting than any man in this city, and he won't act.

DAMON

I won't even get up.

WESTON

Retired! Why have you retired?

KENDALL

I said we lose faith. I mean in our own usefulness. We keep people alive. Yes. But what for? When some silly, overfed woman would come running to me with her symptoms, I'd find myself thinking: "What of it? Suppose you die? Who's going to be any the worse for that?" And the trouble is a doctor can't afford such thoughts. Mine must have shown in my eyes. By the time I came to retire from practice, I didn't have so much practice to retire from.

DAPHNE

Play "Stormy Weather." (*As he starts to play it she boards the song*) "Stormy Weather!"

DAMON

Oh, for God's sake!

MISS TEMPLE

(*Coming in with a tray for* BARRY)

What dreadful music! (*She carries the tray to the piano*) If you're going to curry favor with me, young man, you'll have to play something that wasn't written last Tuesday.

KENDALL

He wouldn't know our tunes, Martha.

BARRY

Oh, I know some of the old songs. (*He lets his hands drift for a moment on the keys, and then begins to play and sing "A Long, Long Trail A-Winding."*)

MISS TEMPLE

Do you call that old? The war was 1914.

BARRY

It's old to me. I was only five then.

MISS TEMPLE

Good Lord, I guess you were!

DAMON
(*From his couch*)
Noel Coward was only four.
(*There follows a bit of haphazard community singing.*
WESTON, THE DOCTOR, MISS TEMPLE *know most of the
words;* BARRY, DAMON, JESSICA *and* DAPHNE *coming in
strong on the refrain.* HATTIE, *coming in to collect* JES-
SICA's *tray, seems disposed to remain for the party.*)

MISS TEMPLE
"No, we're not going to do "The Old Apple Tree." (HATTIE
*retreats. Towards the end of the refrain, there's a ring from
the telephone*) I'll go. Stop, people! (*She takes the receiver off
the hook*) Hello! (*With a gesture*) Stop that noise! (*The
music drops obediently to a hum*) Hello! Hello! ... Yes, this
is 4135. Who do you want? ... Mr. Who? ... Who? (*She is
startled, distressed*) No! There's nobody here of that name. ...
You must have the wrong number. There's nobody here of
that name. (*She hangs up with decision, but stands with her
hand still resting on the telephone.*)

JESSICA
(*Who has been near enough to catch the tone*)
What's the matter, Aunt Martha?

MISS TEMPLE
(*Staring at* JESSICA *a moment*)
Nothing. It was a wrong number.

WESTON
Well, people, I'm sorry to take your one good baritone out
of this ensemble, but I've got to get up in the morning. (MISS
TEMPLE, *having recovered her powers of locomotion, starts*

45

across the room towards DAMON) But first, if the overture is finished, I've got an announcement to make. (*The music peters out.* MISS TEMPLE *has reached the couch and touched* DAMON *on the shoulder.*)

MISS TEMPLE
Damon! (*But he has sat up to listen to* WESTON.)

WESTON
If it's all right with our star, I'd like to bring "The Dark Tower" into New York a week from Monday night.

JESSICA
(*Delighted*)
Oh, Ben, really? Will your theatre be ready?

WESTON
It's ready now. We could give a midnight performance.

JESSICA
Ben, I'm so pleased! (*She throws her arms around his neck and kisses him.*)

WESTON
Say, I wish I'd offered to bring it in this Monday.

BARRY
A week from Monday. That's only nine days off.

DAPHNE
You've made my landlady very happy.

JESSICA
Ben, you can't know what this does for me. I didn't want to worry you all, but I've been terrified of the next four weeks. I had worked my courage up, only to face this let down. But

46

if it's only a week! A week! (*She looks swiftly at* DAMON)
Who's going to play Damon's part?

WESTON

Well—

DAMON

(*Getting up*)

Who do you think's going to play Damon's part? *I* am!

JESSICA

Damon!

BARRY

Say!

DAMON

Oh, what the hell! It's easier to play it than to teach some
other ham how to. Besides, why should I be the only person
I never broke a promise to?

WESTON

I give up. Doctor, I suppose you'll be resuming practice to-
morrow.

JESSICA

I'm so happy. I'm unbelievably happy. Lord help me. I'm
afraid I feel a speech coming on. I do. It's in the blood. Where's
that landing? (*As she goes up the stairs, there's a ripple of
applause, a few cheers, some chords from* BARRY, *who then
dashes from the piano so he can watch her. Altogether, enough
jolly commotion to bring* HATTIE *in from the kitchen. From
the landing,* JESSICA *spreads out her arms in an all-embracing
gesture*) "My constituents." (*To* BARRY) One of the lesser Bar-
ries. Oh, my dears, my dears, I'm a very grateful woman.
Every one that I hold dear is in this room. It's like sitting by

47

a fireside, I feel so warm and protected. Old friends, Doctor, Aunt Martha, Hattie, what would I ever have done without you? Cheer up, Aunt Martha, you look as if you'd seen a ghost. Barry, darling, I thank you for your lovely play. I hope I shall deserve it of you. Ben, dear Ben, what a snug harbor you are for a craft that's known some pretty stormy weather.

DAPHNE
(*A little subdued*)
"Stormy Weather."

DAMON
Shut up!

JESSICA
And Damon, dear brother. Don't scowl and glower at me. Dearest brother ever a girl had, I have no words to tell you what you've been to me. You taught me to walk, and to-day I can't walk without you. I cannot tell you, I can never tell you— (*She wavers and breaks down a little. There is a ring at the doorbell. There are encouraging cries of "Hear, hear!" She is laughing and crying at her own collapse*) Oh, dear! I guess this was one of my mistakes. Barry, you should have written this for me. I should have had a rehearsal. (*There is a second and more insistent ring of the doorbell*) Damon, you should have staged it. I am—

BARRY
(*As* HATTIE *starts forward automatically*)
Shall I—

STANLEY VANCE
(*His voice heard as the door opens*)
Does Miss Jessica Wells still live here? (JESSICA *is transfixed by the voice;* DAMON, MISS TEMPLE, HATTIE *and the* DOCTOR *are*

48

*troubled by it in varying degrees of recognition. There is an
indistinct murmur of voices in the vestibule, wherein one can
distinguish* BARRY *saying "Yes, she does," and* VANCE *saying
"Bring them right in." Enter* STANLEY VANCE. *He is a marked-
down gigolo, in the middle forties, fishbelly-white in complex-
ion. He looks battered. His clothes, of which the coat and
trousers do not match, have been slept in in day-coaches. His
hat is a stained fedora, which he takes off with a bit of manner
as he finds himself, unexpectedly, in the presence of company.
He is followed first by a* TAXI DRIVER, *carrying a bulging cheap
suitcase and a small glass cage, covered with a cloth hood.*
BARRY *comes next and stands uncertainly in the doorway)*
Don't let me disturb any one. Jessica, my bride, as lovely as
ever. Who can let me have a dollar for this fellow?

> (BARRY *and* DAPHNE *are all eyes, interested, puzzled. Now*
> JESSICA, *too, has seen a ghost. The others, each hearing
> the fall of a house of cards, remain rooted in their
> tracks.)*

BARRY

Yes, of course. (*He hauls out some bills, peels off a dollar,
hands it to* VANCE, *who bestows it on the driver. The luggage
has been put down.*)

VANCE

Keep the change. (*The* DRIVER *goes*) Well, here we are!
(*This in a jovial voice as he claps his hands together*) What?
(*With a glance towards the window*) No lamp kept burning
in the window?

> (JESSICA *has started a somnambulistic walk, down the
> stairs, her right hand held a little in front of her, her
> eyes never again, in this act or the next, removed from*

49

him. When she is quite close to him, she touches him once, twice, gropingly on the chest.)

JESSICA

They told me you were dead.

VANCE

(He has watched her with anxious intentness until this moment; when he takes both her hands in his and kisses them. Then, at something he sees in her, he gives the sudden laugh of one who now knows where he stands. You can see his spirits rise and hereafter he is as merry as a grig.)

Ah, the rascals! Maybe the wish was father to the thought. (DAMON *starts forward and pauses helplessly. There is an uneasy movement in the room. As* VANCE *kisses her hands and releases her, she backs uncertainly and sinks into a seat)* Dear, dear, I trust I'm not putting a damper on your little party. Am I not to be introduced? My name—as a rule—is Stanley Vance, prince consort of this fair and somewhat startled lady. You might call me Enoch Arden. I envy you, as spectators, the drama of this return.

BARRY
(Stammering)

I'm afraid—if you don't mind—it's pretty late—I've got to— *(He rushes out.)*

> *(DAPHNE looks to DAMON for instructions, gets them in a dismissive wave and starts for the door.)*

VANCE
(Halting her)

Oh, hello, there! Of course! You're in the play. I saw it to-night. You're really quite good. But in the scene with the

50

husband in the second act—I'm sure you'll pardon me—do you suppose you could give it just a touch of refinement? (*She looks at him with sheer malevolence and walks out*) I'm afraid she couldn't.

WESTON

(*To* DAMON)

Call me in about an hour. (*He gets his hat from the piano, looks unhappily at the group, decides there's nothing he can say, and goes out. He would say good night to* JESSICA, *but she does not know he's in the room.*)

VANCE

(*With a gusty sigh of relief as at something accomplished*)

Ah, I begin to feel the restraint lifting. Strangers are a bit trying at these reunions. (*A meaning look at the* DOCTOR.)

KENDALL

Do you want me, Damon?

DAMON

(*Whose eyes, like* JESSICA's, *have never left* VANCE)

Not to-night.

KENDALL

Good night, Martha.

MISS TEMPLE

Good night, Doctor.

KENDALL

Good night, Jessie.

VANCE

(*After a moment of silence*)

Say good night to the doctor, my dear.

JESSICA

(*without looking at the doctor*)

Good night.

(*The* DOCTOR *goes out. There is the sound of the front door closing.*)

VANCE

That's better. What a comfort for the weary wanderer to find his old chair still waiting by the fireside! (*He settles down*) Hattie! (*She looks vainly to* MISS TEMPLE *for instructions, and comes hesitantly forward*) Still here, eh, Hattie? I sometimes think you should be replaced by some one more nimble, and with perhaps a shade more chic. A glass of milk, Hattie, and— let me see—some white bread, a pat of butter and a bit of cheese.

MISS TEMPLE

(*Galvanized to action*)

Don't you do it, Hattie! Don't you stir! Stanley Vance, get out of this house! Clear out! Kick him out, Damon!

DAMON

(*Quieting her with a gesture and speaking softly*)

Take it easy. Get what he wants, Hattie. (HATTIE *goes out with quickening pace.* DAMON *walks forward, puts a hand under* JESSICA'S *elbow and leads her gently to the seat beneath the landing. He draws her vacated chair towards him and stands with one foot resting on it*) We must get better acquainted, Vance, you and I.

VANCE

Good! And high time, too! As I recall, when Jessica first led her bridegroom home, you weren't exactly cordial. You certainly lost no time in clearing out.

DAMON

I grant you that was a mistake. This time I rather think I'll stick around.

VANCE

Mind you, I wasn't miffed. I understood perfectly. You were so intimate, you and Jessica, you would have resented any man who had full access to her. It accounts for much that we heard later. Rumors that you were drowning yourself in drink—news items borne on the wind from various gutters. Yes—you were a little rude to me, but I forgave you long ago.

DAMON

We thought you were dead. We heard you'd been shot in San Francisco.

VANCE

Yes, that story did get about. I believe it even got into print. It so happened that at the moment I found the rumor not inconvenient. My affairs were in a rather tangled state. Of course, I hated to think of you all grieving, but I was in no position to send a reassuring wire. Well, perhaps it was all for the best. Otherwise, dear brother-in-law, we might have missed the full flavor of this sentimental occasion. (*As* HATTIE *enters*) And here is Peter Pan, tottering in with my frugal meal. (*He draws up his chair to the table*) You can put it here, Hattikins. There we are. It looks delicious. And now, if you will be so good, fetch me my beloved traveling companions. They're over there on the floor beside my suitcase. I promised them on the train that a good home was awaiting us. Be careful with them. They're so sensitive. (HATTIE *handles the cage in gingerly fashion, depositing it at last on the table in front of him*) Here we are. (*He lifts off the hood, revealing a pair of white mice*)

That will be all for to-night, Hattie. You may go. (*She backs away and takes herself off through the dining-room door. For a moment,* VANCE *is engrossed with the feeding of his pets, mumbling endearments, chuckling with pleasure*) Pardon me! Abelard and Heloise, meet the folks. Aunt Martha, let me allay your fears. I can assure you that your house will not be over-run. Abelard has painfully earned his right to be so called. They *are* charming, aren't they?

DAMON

If I remember rightly, they are particularly consoling to men in prison.

VANCE

(*He is busy feeding his mice, and he answers all taunts with invincible good humor*)

Now, how did you know that?

DAMON

Where was it? Out west?

VANCE

San Quentin. A tedious place. I left there Christmas Eve.

DAMON

Bad checks, would be my guess.

VANCE

Very bad. Dear, dear, we've reached the confidential stage. And what have *you* been up to? By the way, I saw the play to-night. (*He settles down to his supper*) Very good. Jessica, of course, superb. A genuine talent. And you were very good. Capital. Yes, all in all, I think we have a success on our hands.

DAMON

Was that what raised you from the dead—this play?

54

VANCE

Well, I'd been feeling for some time I ought to come on. Then, by the merest chance—I was in a barber shop in Oklahoma City—I picked up a New York newspaper. There it was —quite a long article. Jessica Wells returning to the stage. Try-out in Greenwich, everything. So— (*with a wave to his pets*)—we came on.

DAMON

You got here to-day?

VANCE

Yesterday. My apologies—I wanted to go out last night, but I had some business on—was there a telephone call for me?

DAMON

No.

MISS TEMPLE

Yes. (VANCE *looks at her expectantly*) Just before you came.

VANCE

Good. Did he leave a number?

MISS TEMPLE

I hung up.

VANCE

(*A little annoyed*)

I do wish you hadn't done that. Hereafter please see that all messages for me are written down. (*The clock strikes one*) Well— (*With a yawn*) I don't know about you people, but I need my sleep. I think I'll turn in. (*Pushing his chair back and gathering up the mice.*)

MISS TEMPLE

(*Moving forward and taking charge without protest from* DAMON)

55

Just a minute, Stanley Vance! If you think you're going to spend even one night in this house, you're vastly mistaken!

VANCE

Am I?

MISS TEMPLE

Let me remind you that this is my house! You found that out long ago, when you tried to sell it. It's my house and you get out of it!

VANCE

That's final? (*A pause. He shrugs his shoulders*) Ah, well! (*He turns and starts towards the door*) Are you ready, Jessica? (*A pause. She rises uncertainly*) Get your hat, dear. And an overnight bag. And whatever cash you have.

> (*There is a pause as* JESSICA, *wavering like a sleepwalker, turns and starts slowly up the stairs.* MISS TEMPLE, *defeated, sinks into a chair.*)

DAMON

(*Whose eyes have never left* VANCE)

Tell her to stop!

VANCE

(*With a smile*)

Stop, dear.

DAMON

You win the first round.

VANCE

I hoped you'd reconsider. Have we the same old room, Aunt Martha? Here, my dear, guard my treasures. (*He hands* JESSICA *the cage*) Be very careful. (*He starts back for his suitcase*) Really, this is a nuisance, carrying one's own bag. It all comes

56

of having a feeble old woman instead of a proper manservant. (*He joins* JESSICA *at the foot of the stairs*) Say good night, dear.

JESSICA
(*On the landing*)

Good night.

VANCE
(*As he crosses the landing*)

Nighty-night. (*As they vanish up the dark well of the stairway, the silence is broken by* MISS TEMPLE *bursting into tears and sobbing uncontrollably.* DAMON *reaches out a comforting hand to pat her on the shoulder, but he does this abstractedly, for his thoughts have followed his sister and her husband to the floor above.*)

Curtain

ACT TWO

ACT TWO

Scene I

THE HOUSE

One week has elapsed. It is eleven o'clock on Saturday morning. Sunlight streams in from the windows. The clock is striking eleven. After the curtain has risen HATTIE *comes down the stairs, holding at arm's length and with obvious distaste the home of Abelard and Heloise. Her expression is grimly vindictive. She is heading for the dining-room when the telephone rings. After a second's hesitation, she starts for the telephone, carrying the cage with her and taking off the receiver with her free hand.*

HATTIE

Hello! ... Hello! ... No, Mr. Damon ain't here.... Yes, I'll tell him. Wait a minute. (*She rests the cage on the floor, frees her right hand by holding the receiver in her left, and takes up a pencil*) How do you spell it? ... S-A-R-M— What? ... Oh, N. for Nobody—S-A-R-N-O-F-F. Oh, yes, Mr. Sarnoff.... Well, I'll tell him, but he isn't around much. I don't think he lives here any more. (*She hangs up, tucks the memo under the phone, picks up the cage and starts for the dining-room again. The doorbell rings. She answers it.*)

DR. KENDALL

Good morning, Hattie.

HATTIE

Hello, Doctor.

61

DR. KENDALL
(Entering)

Miss Martha in? (*As* HATTIE *follows him in, he notices the mice*) Bless my soul, what's all this? Are they yours?

HATTIE

Mine? I hate them. They belong to that mouse-lover upstairs.

MISS TEMPLE
(Coming down the stairs, dressed for the street)

That the doctor? Oh, thank the Lord. I was just coming across to see you. Who was that on the phone, Hattie?

HATTIE
(On her way out)

It was for Mr. Damon.

MISS TEMPLE
(Sinking down on the end of the couch)

Thank you for coming, doctor. I'm desperate. Damon seems to have deserted us. I don't know what to do.

KENDALL

There's been no change?

MISS TEMPLE

Only for the worse. She slips further and further away. I try to talk to her. I don't think she hears me.

KENDALL

She doesn't.

MISS TEMPLE

It's been a ghastly week. I can't stand much more of it. She's like a person walking in a mist on the edge of a cliff. Do I have to sit and watch her go over the edge?

(DR. KENDALL *rises with a sigh and starts to pace the floor in thought. It is he who first sees* JESSICA *on her way downstairs. She is wearing a plain bathrobe. Her hair has the disorder of Ophelia's. Her expression is the worried, preoccupied conscientious look of a child going on an errand.* STANLEY VANCE'S JESSICA *bears little outward resemblance to the Jessica Wells who played in "The Dark Tower." The freedom of gesture, the vocal color, the very walk are different. This present* JESSICA *has the unvarying manner of a somnambulist, the monotonous voice, the trance quality.*

MISS TEMPLE *sees the* DOCTOR's *glance and she herself turns and rises. The* DOCTOR *goes forward, meeting* JESSICA *at the foot of the stairs, and taking both of her unresisting hands in his.*)

KENDALL

How are you, my dear? I want to talk to you.

JESSICA

I have to see about his breakfast.

KENDALL

Of course you must. But first let me see how you are.

JESSICA

The toast must be thin and buttered. Buttered while it's hot.

KENDALL

But won't you let me talk to you?

JESSICA

I must hurry! I must hurry!

63

KENDALL
(*With intensity*)
What about Ben? What about Damon?

JESSICA
(*In terror*)
He'll be angry! He'll be angry!
(JESSICA *breaks loose and runs to the pantry. There i*
a pause as the DOCTOR *stands looking meditatively afte*
her.)

MISS TEMPLE
Well?

KENDALL
(*After another pause*)
She's like a woman walking in her sleep. It's as though sh
were under ether. That isn't Jessica.

MISS TEMPLE
Will we ever find her again? How shall we look for her?

KENDALL
I'm too old to pretend I know. Of course, I could call a cor
sultation of all the bright young minds at the Medical Center
They'd love it. There used to be some doctors who would hav
understood it. But they're all dead. They died in the Middl
Ages. They would have said she was possessed.

MISS TEMPLE
Possessed!
(JESSICA, *intent, oblivious, hurries in from the dining*
room, runs up the stairs and out of sight.)

KENDALL
And they would have been right.

64

MISS TEMPLE

What are we to do?

KENDALL

Where is Damon?

MISS TEMPLE

God knows! The night that man returned, Damon spent the
night on that couch. I couldn't get him to go upstairs. Since
then I've hardly seen him.

KENDALL

He hasn't slept here?

MISS TEMPLE

No, but that's nothing unusual.

KENDALL

That Martin girl, is it now?

MISS TEMPLE

I suppose so. It's always some one. But he's come to the
house only twice all week. That's not like him. Both times I
tried to talk to him, but he wouldn't pay any attention to me.
He'd look right through me as if he were thinking of something else. How *could* he be thinking of anything else? How
could he be?

KENDALL

Has he been drinking again?

MISS TEMPLE

I saw no signs of it. But the whole thing is so strange. I don't
know which way to turn. What's to be done?

KENDALL

There *is* a remedy, but it isn't in my satchel. I must see

Damon. It's a matter for the police power, really. I don't happen to know the procedure. A visit to some judge in his chambers, I should think, a court order for a committee of her person. After all, it *is* a matter of life and death. Whatever his hold on her may be—

KENDALL

VANCE

(*Coming down the stairs in full regalia. He wears, over shirt and trousers, a flowing Japanese robe of ribbed ivory-colored silk, with a severely simple design of black dragons on it. He wears house-slippers of patent leather. He has the morning papers under his arm.*)

Up and about already? You people must rise at the crack of dawn. All right, Hattie! (*This in a loud voice*) Glad you dropped in, Doctor. I wish you'd take a look at Jessica. It seems to me she's a little peaked. She looks poorly, as my mother used to say. After all, this play's got to open, you know. It's all nonsense, this postponement on her account. These actresses aren't happy when they're not working. Don't you agree with me?

KENDALL

I only caught a glimpse of her. You might send her over later.

VANCE

Incidentally, I'm not feeling quite up to snuff myself. A little bilious, probably. Tell me, is my tongue coated?

KENDALL

(*As* VANCE *sticks out his tongue, peers at it professionally and nods with satisfaction*)

Yes, it is.

VANCE

I thought so. What shall I take?

66

KENDALL

(*Gaily*)

I'm so sorry. I've retired from practice. (*Turns to* MISS TEMPLE) Are you going along now, Martha?

MISS TEMPLE

Yes, but I don't want to miss Damon. (*To* HATTIE, *who has just come in with the breakfast tray*) If Mr. Damon comes in, tell him Dr. Kendall wants to see him. Tell him to go right over.

(MISS TEMPLE *and the* DOCTOR *go out, as* HATTIE *comes down to the table and places the breakfast tray.*)

VANCE

(*Sitting contentedly at his breakfast*)

Jessica, dear, come down here, please. (*To* HATTIE) And now where are my little white companions? They, too, must have their breakfie.

(HATTIE *gives him a dirty look and vanishes into the pantry as* JESSICA *comes down the stairs.*)

VANCE

(*Who has begun to eat his breakfast, with one of the newspapers propped behind his coffee-pot*)

Jessica, my dear, we must stir up this manager of yours. Still nothing in the papers about the play. No ad. No date set for the opening. Do you know his number?

JESSICA

Yes, Stanley.

VANCE

Splendid. Suppose you get him on the phone, will you? (*She starts towards the telephone*) Tell him— (*His voice halts her*) —tell him you'd like to see him, and ask him to pop in

67

here as soon as possible. Remember *you* want to see him. (*She goes on to the telephone and dials obediently. In the ensuing intervals he continues to coach her*) Just be casual. We mustn't let him think we're anxious about it.

JESSICA

Is Mr. Weston in? (*A pause*) This is Jessica Wells.

VANCE

Now be cheerful, bright. Just say you'd like to see him and find out how soon he can come up.

JESSICA

Hello, Ben. This is Jessica. (*Pause*) Oh, I'm fine. (*Pause*) No, I'm all right.

> (VANCE, *listening intently, gets up with his napkin in one hand and a piece of toast in the other, and goes over behind her.*)

Well, it's good to hear your voice, too. Ben, I'd like to have a talk with you about the play.

VANCE

> (*With a gesture bidding her keep the tone up*)

Gayer! Brighter! Laugh!

> (JESSICA *gives a forlorn attempt at a gay laugh.*)

JESSICA

Oh, will you? Right away? (*She gives a glance at* VANCE *for instructions. You can see him forming the words, "That's all" with his lips*) Yes, that's all. That will be fine. (*She gives another nervous little laugh and hangs up.*)

VANCE

> (*Leaning over and picking up the recently written memo, he gives a glance at it, tosses it back*)

68

Now run upstairs and put on a nice dress. (*Returning to his breakfast*) Fix your hair. It's all straggly. (*He takes a big bite of toast.*)

> (HATTIE *enters, with the mouse-cage in one hand and a carpet-sweeper in the other. She is fearfully arrayed for house-cleaning, a dust-cloth wound around her head, her person enveloped in a vast outer-apron. She rests the sweeper against the wall and deposits the cage on the table. She retrieves her sweeper and starts cleaning up-stage.*)

> (*Examining the cage critically*)

Not any too clean, Hattie. You didn't do a very good job with this.

HATTIE
(*Sweeping furiously*)
I'm a housekeeper, not a mouse-keeper.

VANCE
After breakfast, I must ask you to do it over. (*She sweeps still more furiously.* VANCE *starts to feed the mice, at the same time addressing them with a genuine and tender affection no human ever elicits from him*) Hello, you little rascals! How's your appetite? Want the regular club breakfast? Now, there, Abelard, you mustn't be grabby. Let Heloise have her share. That's the trouble with you capons. No chivalry. That's better. Well, Mam'zelle, and how are you feeling this fine Summer morning? (*He sings to them softly "Two Blind Mice," letting the words subside into a mere humming. Meanwhile* HATTIE *has begun to take his vicinity into the orbit of her sweeping. Several times the sweeper bumps into the chair. At first, he mechanically shifts his chair, but this doesn't satisfy* HATTIE.

69

Finally her efforts are rewarded. He turns on her with an explosion) What the hell are you doing there?

HATTIE

I can't help it if you sleep all day and then come down here while I'm cleaning.

(HATTIE *gives another thrust with the sweeper.*)

VANCE

Listen, you old crone, once I get the idea that you're *trying* to be a nuisance, one of us will have to leave this house.

HATTIE

That suits me.

VANCE

I'd put you on the streets, my pretty one, but I don't think you'd be much of a success.

HATTIE

(*Taking up a position of defiance with her hands clasped on her sweeper*)
Now you listen to me, you big pimp—

(*There's a ring at the door.* HATTIE *suspends hostilities and* VANCE *resumes his seat as she goes to the door, depositing the sweeper en route, and divesting herself of her cap and second apron as she goes.*)

DAPHNE
(*Heard in the hall*)
Is Mr. Wells home?

HATTIE

No, he isn't.

DAPHNE

Well, is *Miss* Wells here?

70

HATTIE

Well, I'll have to see.

VANCE

Who's that?
> (DAPHNE, *construing this as an invitation, barges in past*
> HATTIE.)

Oh, hello, there.

DAPHNE

Hello. You still here?

VANCE

I seem to be.

DAPHNE

Maybe you can tell me what I want to know.

HATTIE

Don't you want Miss Wells?
> (*There's another ring of the doorbell.* HATTIE *responds.*)

DAPHNE
> (*Seeing the mice*)

For God's sake, where did you get the polar bears? Did you
catch them?

VANCE

I charmed them.
> (*A voice at the door asks* "*Vance?*" VANCE *turns to listen
> as* HATTIE *comes in with a big, smart-looking box, which
> she promptly deposits against the wall.*)

HATTIE

For you. (*She scoops up her sweeper and starts for the dining-
room.*)

71

VANCE

(*Mildly*)

Hattie, didn't you say something about giving the cage another cleaning?

HATTIE

(*Gathering up the cage with considerable bitterness and starting for the dining-room*)

What this house needs is a good cat.

VANCE

Hattie! (*Halting her by the tone of his voice*) If you vent your spleen against me on those innocent creatures, so help me God I'll knock you down and gouge your eyes out. (HATTIE *goes.*)

DAPHNE

Tough guy, eh?

VANCE

(*A little apologetic and quite genuine*)

I can't stand the idea of any one being cruel to animals. Now, then, what's on your mind?

DAPHNE

On my mind? A man named Wells and a play called "The Dark Tower." Say, where's he been all week?

VANCE

Am I my brother-in-law's keeper?

DAPHNE

No. (*With a glance at his opulence*) Looks to me as if it's the other way around.

VANCE

Now, now, don't be cross with me just because our Damon has escaped your bed and board

72

DAPHNE

Look! Has he been here?

VANCE

Infrequently, I'm afraid. (*Rising and collecting his box, bringing it forward and opening it up. To cut the string, he draws out from his trouser-pocket a knife with a long, spring blade.*)

DAPHNE

Well, where's he living?

VANCE

Who knows? You're an irresponsible lot, you theatrical people. Your boy friend is like the rest of you—a bird of passage.

DAPHNE

When I catch him, I'll wring his neck!
(*By this time,* VANCE *has drawn from their tissue-wrappings a half-dozen pairs of monogrammed pajamas in silks of various pastel shades.* DAPHNE *vouchsafes them a mild snort.*)

VANCE

(*Running through his finery*)
Black on blue. That's right. Corn-color, black on green, white with blue monogram, gun-metal with white monogram, powder-blue on old— Now look at that! I told them old rose and what do they give me?

DAPHNE

Buckwheats?

VANCE

No, but seriously— (*As he starts putting them back in the*

box) it's impossible to get anything done *right* any more. Well, I shall have to send them back, that's all.

DAPHNE

I wish I had your troubles. What I want to know is whether this play's ever going to open. When do I go on salary?

VANCE

Ah, who can tell? Meanwhile keep up in your part. "We know neither the day nor the hour when the bridegroom cometh!"

(*There is the sound of the front door opening and closing, a pause—and then* DAMON *lounges into sight, his hat on the back of his head. He stands for a moment leaning against the door-jamb, his hands in his pocket.*)

DAMON

(*Looking always at* VANCE)

Well, a new grouping.

DAPHNE

Where the hell have you been?

DAMON

That, my dear, will come out in my memoirs.

DAPHNE

You've left me flat for a week.

DAMON

Well, that's the way I found you.

DAPHNE

I know more than you think I do. What were you doing in Philadelphia last Monday?

74

DAMON
(*After a barely perceptible pause*)
You must be mistaken. I never go to Philadelphia.

DAPHNE
I know better. I know some one that saw you. It's the first time anybody's walked out on me and gone to Philadelphia.

DAMON
I said you were mistaken.

DAPHNE
Yeah? Well, then, I'll tell you something I'm *sure* of, and that's Wednesday afternoon.

DAMON
(*Looking her way for the first time and cutting in with an intensity that scares her*)
Shut your mouth and get out of here!

DAPHNE
(*Startled*)
Why, honey—

DAMON
Run along, I tell you!

DAPHNE
But—but what about the play, Damon?

DAMON
I'll call you to-morrow.

DAPHNE
But I've been waiting all week—

75

DAMON
(*Between clenched teeth*)
I'll call you to-morrow.

DAPHNE
(*A little dazed*)
So long. (*She summons her accustomed spirit, and, as she approaches the door, remembers the silk pajamas and delivers a parting shot at* VANCE) And good-by to you, you big pansy!

VANCE
(*Sitting as for a conference*)
Glad you dropped in, Wells. I want to talk to you.

DAMON
Where's Jessica?

VANCE
Upstairs.

DAMON
Where's my aunt?

VANCE
Gone out. Look here, Wells. What about this play? When's it going to open?

DAMON
That's up to you.

VANCE
(*With spurious surprise*)
Up to me?

DAMON
Shall I make myself clear?

VANCE
Pray do.
76

DAMON

Normally, my sister is, I think, the most promising young actress in America. When you're around, she turns into a colorless automaton I wouldn't trust with the job of carrying a tray across the stage.

VANCE

Yes, that would happen to me, wouldn't it? I marry the most promising young actress in America and the little woman goes to pot on me. Damned annoying.

DAMON

There's one thing I'd like to ask you. This may be my last chance.

VANCE

Don't tell me we're not going to meet again?

DAMON

Oh, yes, we'll meet again. But here's what puzzles me. Why do you kill the goose that lays your golden egg?

VANCE

I do, don't I? I'm an impractical creature, I guess.

DAMON

No. I think not. It seems out of character. Do you do it deliberately?

VANCE

(*Ruminatively*)

No. No. I don't enjoy this sort of thing—living with any one so spineless. Frankly, meek women bore me. I like something with a little spirit—more like that— (*With a gesture that recalls* DAPHNE) Say, she's pretty good. Oh, I won't say it isn't sort of fun for a while—reducing a woman to putty. Any man

77

enjoys that. Feeds the male vanity. That night I came back, for instance—to walk in here shabby, uncertain, not knowing where my next meal was coming from, all of you hating me— it did sort of tickle me to find out I was still the ringmaster, that your precious Jessica would still jump through hoops for me. And I'll admit this, too. I enjoy watching all you helpless onlookers wriggle and squirm, wishing to God I'd fall and break my pretty neck. It *is* fun, but—(*ruefully*)—of course, it butters no parsnips.

HATTIE
(*Drawn by the voices*)

Oh, Mr. Damon. Dr. Kendall was here and Miss Martha said if you came in, would you go right over and see him?

(DAMON *nods.*)

VANCE

It seems there's to be a conference. They're going into a huddle.

HATTIE
(*Gathering up* VANCE's *tray*)

Finished with this?

VANCE
(*Nodding*)

To-morrow, squeeze a grape-fruit into that orange juice.

HATTIE

And oh, yes, Mr. Damon. That foreign gentleman, Mr. Sarnoff, called up again. I put a note over there.

DAMON

Thanks.

(HATTIE *goes out.*)

78

VANCE

Well, there you are. You might report to the conference that the situation is unchanged. Your gifted sister belongs to me just as much as that wrist-watch belongs to you.

DAMON

What good does it do you?

VANCE

Well— (*As he slowly weighs the situation*) —I think I may say I have a little nuisance value. My departure should be worth something to some one.

DAMON

That suggestion has a faint aroma of blackmail.

VANCE

Don't be romantic. A straight business proposition. My wife owns half this play. Whoever really wants to see it produced ought to be glad to buy her half from me.

DAMON

For instance?

VANCE

Well, this man Weston. (DAMON *gives a contemptuous snort*) As a matter of fact, he's on his way here right now.

DAMON

Weston won't buy your pretty violets.

VANCE

Why shouldn't he?

DAMON

Why should he? He already owns fifty per cent of a wrecked property! What does he want with the rest of it?

79

VANCE

Oh, come now, not wrecked. Just held up for a while.

DAMON

How do we know it's just for a while?

VANCE

She'll come around as soon as she's deprived of my fascina
tion.

DAMON

How do we know that? She didn't the last time. And an
other thing. Suppose you do go West—back to Oklahoma o
wherever it was.

VANCE

No, I've other plans this time. My fancy rather runs t
Europe.

DAMON

All right. Suppose you go to Europe? Suppose you go t
Thibet? How do we know you'll stay away?

VANCE

Of course, there *is* that.

DAMON

Oh, no! Welcome as your departure would be, welcome as
must always be from wherever you are, I'm afraid it's no
enough. If your mere exit would do the trick, I'd buy you ou
myself.

VANCE

You'd buy me out? With what? I wouldn't settle for sma
change, you know.

80

DAMON

(*Nettled*)

That would be no problem. I could get the money.

VANCE

Where from? Borrow it around the Lambs Club?

DAMON

Oh, I can always get backing. There's a nut been calling me up all over town this week. Showering me with messages, like confetti. He must be a nut—he wants to buy into this show. Of course he doesn't know about you.

VANCE

(*With an involuntary glance towards the telephone*)

What's his name?

DAMON

Wouldn't you like to know?

VANCE

Is it, by any chance, Sarnoff?

DAMON

Ah, been opening my mail, eh?

VANCE

Well, if he's so hot to buy, why don't you introduce me to him?

DAMON

(*With a roar of scorn*)

Introduce *you*? Why, introducing you ought to be declared a felony. Probably is in most states.

VANCE

No, but seriously—

DAMON

"Max Sarnoff, allow me to present my brother-in-law, Stanley Vance, who wants to get some money out of you and doesn't care how he gets it. If you'd like to know his usual method, ask the warden out at San Quentin. If he suggests your going into business with him, I think I ought to warn you there is only one profession at which he's shown any promise. He's an expert in the art of living on women. It's lovely work if you can get it, but of course it takes a certain slimy charm."

VANCE

Getting a little nasty, aren't you?

DAMON

Wait till I'm warmed up. "And furthermore, dear Mr. Sarnoff, it might profit you to consult the Coroner's records in Frederickton, Maryland—" (VANCE *evinces surprise at this shot*) "—for about 1913. You'll find suggestive material in the sudden death of a Mrs. Sarah Applegate Vance, who had carelessly willed her small estate to her inconsolable young husband—"

VANCE

You've been doing a little research, eh?

DAMON
(*Triumphant*)
Then I'm right! It was a shot in the dark, but I'm right!

VANCE
(*With his first signs of anger*)
The verdict was suicide!

DAMON
(*Jubilant*)
And I was only guessing! Her inconsolable young husband

VANCE

She killed herself, I tell you!

DAMON

I wouldn't have blamed her.

VANCE

(*Regaining control of himself with visible effort*)
Anyhow, that's ancient history. You theatrical people are too emotional. You dodge the facts. (*He goes to the stairway and calls up*) Jessica, dear, come here a minute. (*After a pause, she appears*) Our company should be here soon. (*He takes off the robe and hands it to her*) Suppose you bring me my coat and waistcoat. (*He glances at his slippers and adds as she starts to go*) And my low tan shoes and a shoehorn. That's all.

(*JESSICA goes.*)

And now I'm sure you are in a hurry to attend the family conference. Carry this thought with you. I hold the pride of this house in the hollow of my hand. Your cherished sister is my personal property and I can do anything I like with her. (*JESSICA reappears with the articles ordered*) Ah, my dear, that's right! (*He resumes his seat*) And now if you'll be so good as to help an old gentleman complete his toilet. (*Obediently and without looking at* DAMON, *she kneels at* VANCE's *feet and starts putting on his shoes for him.* DAMON *watches this scene in grim silence*) Miss Jessica Wells, who is Mrs. Stanley Vance in private life, in a characteristic pose. (DAMON *turns on his heel and flings out of the house. As the door bangs,* VANCE *clucks disapprovingly*) Dear, dear, what manners! (*A pause as he plans his campaign*) Oh, never mind. (*Impatiently he waves her away and he himself finishes tying his shoes.* JESSICA *gets his coat and vest and stands waiting*) Tell me something. (*He pauses in the tying of a knot*) Do you happen to know a man named Sarnoff?

JESSICA

I don't think so.

VANCE

Max Sarnoff?

JESSICA

No.

VANCE

Think carefully. He's a friend of your brother's. (*She shakes her head*) No one of that name came out to see the play? Didn't come back to your dressing-room?

JESSICA

No, Stanley.

VANCE

(*After an abstracted pause in which he finishes tying his shoe and gets into the vest and coat she holds for him. He crosses with purposeful strides to the telephone and rereads the memo tucked beneath it. Then he goes to the dining-room doorway and calls out.*)

Hattie! Hattie!

HATTIE

I'm bringing them. (*She enters with the cage*) Here!

VANCE

(*Absorbed*)

Hattie, this man Sarnoff that called up. Has he called up here before?

HATTIE

He didn't ask for you. It was for Mr. Damon.

84

VANCE

Well, tell me, you didn't put any number down. Did he say where he could be reached?

HATTIE

No, he didn't.

VANCE

But when he called before?

HATTIE

I don't remember.

VANCE

Nonsense! He must have said something about where he was.

HATTIE

I don't remember.

VANCE

You remember writing his name down, don't you?

HATTIE

No, I don't.

VANCE

Oh, all right! Get out!

HATTIE
(*Holding out the cage*)

Here!

VANCE
(*As he starts for the telephone book*)

Put them anywhere. (HATTIE *puts the cage on the piano and goes out with an air of quiet triumph.* VANCE *sits at the telephone, and runs down the Sarnoff name in the book*) Sarkadi, Sarnelli, Sarno, Sarnoff. Aaron Sarnoff, Charles, David, Helen,

Irving, Morris— (*As he closes the book*) Damn! (*He stands
for a moment thinking fast. Still abstracted, he paces a moment
and then waves an impatient hand at* JESSICA) Sit down. (*He
takes another turn of the room, assembling his plan. Then he
goes swiftly to her, sits on the edge of the table, takes her hand
between his hands*) Now, my girl, see if you can get this into
your head. There's a man who's trying to buy our share of the
play. I don't know where he is yet, but I'll find him. He wants
to pay a lot of money for it. Understand? (*She looks at him
bewildered. He continues in a slightly sharper tone*) Listen!
He won't buy it if he thinks it isn't going right on. And he's
sure to ask Weston *when* it's going on. Do you understand
that?

JESSICA
(*Automatically*)

When it's going on.

VANCE

So more than ever you've got to make Weston think you're
all right. And you *are* all right, aren't you? (*She stares at him
dumbly*) *Aren't* you? (*In despair of reaching her mind, he
pushes her impatiently from him and starts pacing the room*)
Christ! What chance has a fellow explaining anything to you!
You can't think! (*He darts quickly to the window, parts the
curtain, looks out onto the doorstep*) If I only had more time!
He's liable to— (*He controls himself with difficulty, summons
his forces and strides over to her with a decisive movement*)
Now! (*He looks right into her eyes*) You could go right on
that stage Monday night and give a wonderful performance.
You could go right on that stage Monday night and give a
wonderful performance.

86

JESSICA

I could go right on that stage Monday night and give a wonderful performance.

VANCE

You're perfectly well and there's no reason why the play couldn't open to-night. Now, let's hear you say it. "Hello, Jessica."

JESSICA

Hello, Stanley.

VANCE

No! (*Involuntarily slapping her in the face*) "Hello, Ben."

JESSICA

Hello, Ben.

VANCE

"And how are you?"

JESSICA

(*Gathering her forces and giving an excellent performance of her old self*)

I'm all right. Only I'm terribly impatient to get to work.

VANCE

That's fine. "But do you think you can stand the strain?"

JESSICA

Why, Ben, I'm perfectly well. There's no reason why we couldn't open to-night.

VANCE

That's the stuff. Just talk to him pleasantly, naturally. (*He makes a quick dart to the window*) And after you've talked to him a while, I'll come into the room. (*He stations himself at*

87

the window) Now try it again and see how you do it this time. "Hello, Jessica."

JESSICA

Hello, Ben, dear.

VANCE

(*Looking back*)

That's good. That's good.

JESSICA

Oh, Ben, I'm so glad to see you.

VANCE

(*With a snap of his fingers*)

Here he is! (*He hurries over to her and steadies her with a pacifying pressure on her shoulders. Then he darts up to the stairs, catching up his slippers as he goes. There is a ring at the doorbell. As* HATTIE *comes in to answer it, he gives parting instructions from the landing*) Now watch your step, my girl. (*He vanishes up the stairway.*)

WESTON

(*In the hall*)

Hello there, Hattie. I've come to see Miss Jessica. (*You hear* HATTIE *murmuring, "How do you do, Mr. Weston," as he enters. His quick glance sweeps the room. At sight of her, he tosses his hat aside, strides forward and takes both of Jessica's hands in his*) My dear, my dear, let me look at you. (HATTIE, *much interested, crosses and departs reluctantly*) God, what a relief it is to see you! I've been imagining a thousand things! Are you safe? Are you all right?

JESSICA

I'm fine, Ben. I could go on to-night.

WESTON

I've been trying all week to get a word with you. God, how I shook when I heard your voice on the phone just now! It seemed to come from another world. Tell me, Jessica, my dearest, are you all right?

JESSICA

Ben, we could open any time. I can go on.

WESTON

The play! Bless your heart, the play doesn't matter. The hell with the play! It's you I'm thinking about. Jessica, you must get out of here. Let me take you away. Now! This minute!

JESSICA

But the play, Ben. I can go on.

WESTON

Of course you can. We'll talk it all over in the cab—

JESSICA

No! No!

WESTON

Then, don't you see, dear, we'd be on our way out of here. Out of here for good.

JESSICA

Oh, no! Ben, Ben!

WESTON

What are you frightened of? Surely not me. I want to shelter you, Jessica. Let me stand between you and all that's cruel in the world.

JESSICA
(With mounting terror)

We mustn't! We mustn't!

WESTON

You can't *want* to stay with that man. Think! Think! Just a week ago! We were so happy. Remember? (JESSICA, *in her trembling, is beyond forming words*) Jessica, I love you! I've loved you for years! You must have known it! You did know it! You do know it! (*He takes her by the shoulders*) Don't you? Don't you?

JESSICA

(*For one brief moment summoned through the fog. For the first time she really knows him*)

Ben, dearest! Dearest Ben! (*But her fears regain their hold on her*) No, I mustn't! I mustn't! (*She glances in terror towards the stairs.*)

WESTON

You're frightened. What— (*He, too, glances towards the landing; then walks grimly to the foot of the stairs, as she sinks to the couch*) Where are you, Vance? (*A pause*) Come down out of there! (*Another pause. He starts slowly up. As he reaches the landing,* VANCE *emerges.*)

VANCE

(*With a not too successful attempt at casualness*)

Hello, it's Weston! How are you, old man? (WESTON *backs down the stairs and* VANCE *follows him*) I've been wanting to see you. (*He takes elaborate notice of Jessica*) Well, what's this? You seem distressed, my dear. What have you been saying to her, Weston? Perhaps it's just as well I came down when I did.

WESTON

I want a word with you, Vance—alone.

VANCE

(*After a moment's pause*)

Jessica, go to your room. (*With* WESTON *watching her and* VANCE *watching Weston,* JESSICA *goes up the stairs*) Now see here, Weston. I'm just about fed up with this shilly-shally. There must be limits to your right to delay my wife's season. If you don't announce an opening date by Monday, we'll have to drop you out of the picture. As a matter of fact, I'm lining up a new backer right now. I've never liked the idea of messing around the theatre, but you give me no choice.

WESTON

(*Who has been speculatively regarding him as one would any curious phenomenon*)

This is very interesting to me. I'd heard about you, Vance, before you showed up the other night. You were described to me by those who know you as the complete son-of-a-bitch. They didn't tell the half of it. Now I've seen you at work with my own eyes, I think that certain steps are indicated. (*He walks over and picks up his hat*) They'll bear thinking about. There must be a way of putting a person like you where you can't do any more harm. Of course, the best way, I suppose, is just to crunch you underfoot on the sidewalk. Anyway, I think it's fair to warn you that I'm not going to stand by and do nothing about it.

VANCE

You don't frighten me, big shot. I'm on to you. There must be a way of putting a person like you where he can't fool around with another man's wife. You've been sleeping with her and you're just sore because I came back.

WESTON

(*After one look*)

Oh, hell, why wait? (*He tosses his hat on the piano and starts for Vance.*)

VANCE

(*Retreating*)

Keep your hands off! Don't you touch me! I'm warning you! (*He reaches for his knife and springs the blade.* WESTON *jumps for him, catches his right arm, twists it till the knife clatters to the floor, chuckles happily, bends* VANCE *back over the couch and luxuriously starts to choke him. The ring of the doorbell interrupts this pleasurable activity. Slowly* WESTON *releases his gasping victim, confiscates the knife, straightens up and walks away. The bell rings again.* VANCE *is just pulling himself together as* HATTIE *enters, and, with some interest in the subsiding excitement, crosses to open the door.*)

SARNOFF

(*Heard at the door. He speaks with a perceptible Viennese accent*)

Is this the home of Mr. Damon Wells?

HATTIE

Yes, but he isn't here.

SARNOFF

I am so sorry. I have been calling him. My name is Sarnoff.

VANCE

(*His interest caught immediately*)

Sarnoff! Wait a minute, Hattie! (*He starts into the vestibule*) What's that?

92

SARNOFF

I am so sorry. My name is Sarnoff.

VANCE

Well, well—come right in, sir. He'll be here any minute.
(MAX SARNOFF *enters. He is tall, swarthy, foreign-looking.
His bearing is slightly military. He limps. His right arm
is in a black silk sling. His black raincoat is merely
draped over the useless arm. He carries a walking-
stick.*)

VANCE

(*Hovering around him*)
Let me take your hat and coat.

SARNOFF

Thank you, no. I cannot stay.

WESTON

(*Who has retrieved his hat, looks at Vance sardonically*)
I'll be seeing you, Mr. Vance. I'll get in touch with you. Oh,
I seem to have picked up your knife. (*Tosses it on to piano*)
Sorry. (WESTON *goes as* VANCE *nods and involuntarily fingers
his throat. Meanwhile* HATTIE *has gone.*)

VANCE

(*Elaborately placing a chair*)
Sit down, Mr. Sarnoff, sit down. My name is Vance—Stanley
Vance. I'm Mr. Wells's brother-in-law. I've often heard him
speak of you.

SARNOFF

Ah, then you—you are the husband of Miss Jessica Wells?

VANCE

Yes, that is my somewhat humble rôle.

93

SARNOFF

My felicitations. A charming actress.

VANCE

We think so.

SARNOFF

You say you are expecting Mr. Wells?

VANCE

Yes, yes, he'll be here any minute. Do let me take your coat.

SARNOFF

(*Yielding it doubtfully*)

Well, thank you.

(SARNOFF *sits down.*)

VANCE

(*Holding out a cigarette case*)

Smoke?

SARNOFF

No, thank you. It is the one thing I have not been able to learn in this country. I cannot smoke your cigarettes.

VANCE

(*Lighting a cigarette for himself*)

Yes, sir—Great fellow, Damon.

SARNOFF

He seems to be a gifted man. As actor, as director. I saw the play last week in—what was that place?

VANCE

Greenwich. Damon told me about it. The boy generally talks over his little problems with me.

94

SARNOFF

Ordinarily I would not seek out a gentleman in his home on a matter of business, but I could not reach him anywhere and my time is pressing. I am required to leave New York to-night.

VANCE

Then this is a rather happy accident. It's just as well you did come here, Mr. Sarnoff. Why, Damon was telling me just a while ago how he was going to introduce me to you. You see, the most he could do would be to put you in touch with me.

SARNOFF

I am afraid I do not understand.

VANCE

Well, Damon doesn't own any of the play himself. It belongs to my wife—that is, half of it.

SARNOFF
(*Delighted*)

Good! Good! You can speak for Miss Wells?

VANCE

Of course, of course. My wife. Our interests are one.

SARNOFF

Splendid, Mr.—er—

VANCE

Vance.

SARNOFF

Mr. Vance. Now then, Mr. Vance, my situation is this. (*He pauses as the front door, to the visible uneasiness of* VANCE, *is heard to open. They both turn and look as* MISS TEMPLE *comes in from the street. She sees a stranger in conference with* VANCE, *suspects the worst and with set jaw crosses and goes up the steps.*)

VANCE

My wife's aunt. A harmless eccentric.

SARNOFF

(*Sympathetic*)

I understand.

VANCE

(*With a reconnoitering glance up the stairs*)

I'm afraid this isn't a very good place for a conference. Can't we go somewhere else?

SARNOFF

Well, it is not convenient at the moment. I am having *dejeuner* with our consul. But shortly after that—perhaps you would come to my hotel.

VANCE

Yes, yes, of course. About what time, Mr. Sarnoff?

SARNOFF

Hmmm—shall we say three o'clock? I am at the Waldorf.

VANCE

Three o'clock at the Waldorf. That'll be fine. Allow me. (*He helps the visitor into his coat.*)

SARNOFF

(*Fishing in his pocket for a hotel key*)

You will find me in Suite Number— (*He reads from the key-tag*) 1970.

VANCE

Good! Now, do I understand, Mr. Sarnoff, that you will be

in a position to close the transaction this afternoon? I mean since you are going away to-night.

SARNOFF

In a position, most certainly. If we are in agreement on terms. I assume, Mr. Vance, that you will bring to the hotel your credentials. Perhaps—to be quite business-like—a power of attorney from your wife.

VANCE

Oh, to be sure, to be sure.

SARNOFF

Well, *auf wiedersehen,* Mr. Vance. It has been a happy meeting. (*He starts towards the door*) I trust it will prove profitable to both of us.

VANCE

(*Escorting him into the vestibule*)

Good-by, Mr. Sarnoff. Three o'clock at the Waldorf. (*There is the sound of the door closing.* VANCE *prances back into the room, dancing and singing in sheer high spirits. He spies his mouse-cage, catches it up and brings it to the table*) Ah, there, my pretties! It looks as though we're going on a trip. What would you think of that? What would you say to a nice little trip to Europe? Eh, Abelard and Heloise? What would you think of that? Paris. Vienna. The Riviera. Orvieto. Ah, Orvieto, my darlings! Wait till you taste the cheese in Orvieto!

Curtain

ACT TWO

SCENE II

The sitting room of Suite 1970 at the Waldorf. Three doors are in evidence; one leading into the main corridor; one into the closet and one into a bedroom. A table drawn out from the wall and appropriated as a desk is equipped with papers and a desk lamp. Of the four upholstered chairs in the room, one is on either side of this desk. Beside a third chair stands a little table equipped with whisky, decanter, White Rock bottles, glasses, bottle-opener and the like.

At the rising of the curtain MAX SARNOFF *is discovered sitting on one of the chairs near the table. He is dressed as before, save that his discarded hat and raincoat rest on the chair near the door leading to the main corridor. The light from the desk-lamp falls on the notebook and pleasing person of* MISS PATSY DOWLING, *a pretty stenographer—round, soft, stupid and willing. She is taking dictation.*

SARNOFF

"—to help you understand something you may read in tomorrow's newspapers. You at least will realize with what satisfaction I am able to report that at last have I come face to face with our old friend, Stanley Vance. I saw him only a few hours ago. Had quite a chat with him, and he did not recognize me."

MISS DOWLING

Say, what *is* all this?

SARNOFF

"Of course, he, too, had changed, but I would have known him anywhere, and at any time."

MISS DOWLING

I'm getting excited.

SARNOFF

Control yourself, my dear. "I picked up his trail at a theatre in the suburbs a week ago. You may have read in the newspaper that that unfortunate woman he married was about to reappear on the stage. I had an idea that this might draw him from wherever he was. I attended every performance, and had almost given up hope when, on Saturday night, I saw him come in and buy a balcony ticket. It was the end of a long, long hunt, my dear Michael."

MISS DOWLING
(*Admiringly*)

Say, I wouldn't like to be in his shoes!

SARNOFF
(*With a silencing gesture*)

"So, very soon my work will be done. *Auf wiedersehen,* my dear Michael."

MISS DOWLING

Huh? (*Giving him a distracted look.*)

SARNOFF

"Till we meet again, dear Michael." That is all for that one.

MISS DOWLING
(*Flicking back her pages*)

You didn't give me any name and address. You just said "Friend Michael."

SARNOFF

I know—I know.

MISS DOWLING

But what about the envelope?

SARNOFF

I will address the envelope. Will you have the letter typed before I leave, please.

MISS DOWLING

Gee, I hate to think of your going. You've been a good customer.

SARNOFF

Perhaps I will come back sometime. Meanwhile, should you ever come out to the fair city of Tulsa—

MISS DOWLING

(*With a giggle*)

Imagine me in Tulsa! I wouldn't know what to do.

SARNOFF

Same as you do here. It is universal.

MISS DOWLING

(*Her spirits rising*)

Aren't you terrible! Say, how about a little drink?

SARNOFF

No. I think I will need my wits for this meeting.

MISS DOWLING

No, I meant me.

SARNOFF

Not to-day, my child. My supply is a little short.

MISS DOWLING

Oh, I'll just take a little bit of a one. Why not?

SARNOFF

(*Sternly*)

No!

MISS DOWLING

Well, you don't have to bite my head off.

SARNOFF

Better for you not to drink. (*Rising and going towards the closet.*)

MISS DOWLING

I wish you were going to stay one more night. We could see that picture at the Capitol.

SARNOFF

Well, you go without me. (*He opens the closet door, as if experimenting with it. An automatic light appears inside. He shuts the door, locks it, unlocks it. There is a ring at the telephone.*)

MISS DOWLING

Want *me* to?

SARNOFF

Please.

MISS DOWLING

(*At the phone*)

Hello...Yes...Well, just a minute. (*She looks at Sarnoff with snapping eyes and speaks in a stage whisper*) It's that Mr. Vance.

SARNOFF

Tell them to send him up.

102

MISS DOWLING

(*In the telephone*)

Send him up. (*She hangs up*) Can't I stay?

SARNOFF

You run along, my dear. I will see you downstairs. (*She gathers up her notebook and starts for the door.*)

MISS DOWLING

How soon you checking out? When will you want this?

SARNOFF

Oh, I should not be very long. Let us say—ten or fifteen minutes.

MISS DOWLING

Well, see you later. (*She goes out.*)

(*Left alone,* SARNOFF *takes a swift glance around the room, crosses to the door through which she has just left, taking his right arm from the sling as he does so, and rattles the knob to make sure the door is tightly closed. Next he limps swiftly into the bedroom, to reappear a few seconds later with a towel, which, after a slight hesitation, he carries to the closet and places on a shelf within. Then he closes the closet door. Next he straightens up the papers on his table, and, pulling open a drawer, takes out of it a stiletto, which he examines critically, hefts, flexes and then places thoughtfully back in the drawer. Then, slipping his arm back into the sling, he comes around to Miss Dowling's chair, sits on it and fixes a steady gaze on the door. There is a painful pause, followed by a knock on the door. He crosses slowly to open it. Enter* VANCE, *followed by* JESSICA. *She is for the first time dressed with striking chic. She has been costumed for a killing.*)

VANCE

Well, Mr. Sarnoff, right on time. Jessica, my dear, let me present Mr. Max Sarnoff. Mr. Sarnoff, you suggested that I bring my credentials. Here they are.

SARNOFF

(*Ever so slightly taken aback*)

Charmed, Madame Vance. I have long admired you from a distance, but your visit is a most unexpected— (*Pause*)—honor. Pray be seated, Madame. (*He indicates the easy-chair by the table*) And you, sir.

VANCE

Well, you're certainly high enough up here.

SARNOFF

(*Bowing Jessica into her seat, being careful the while to keep his left hand behind him*)

Yes, it is a rare treat for us Europeans to be lodged so high.

VANCE

I told my wife you were interested in the play, Mr. Sarnoff, and nothing would do but she must come along and meet you. Eh, dear?

JESSICA

Yes, Stanley.

SARNOFF

I think it is a most distinguished play. And your performance, Madame Vance, of course—so sympathetic.

JESSICA

I think it's a beautiful play. We were all so happy in it. I can't believe it was only last week.

VANCE
(*Breaking in nervously*)

No doubt about it, she's a born actress, Mr. Sarnoff. Never really happy when the curtain isn't up. Just children, they are, these people of the theatre. Fortunately, she has me to look after her business interests.

SARNOFF

Fortunate, indeed.

VANCE
(*Reaching in his pocket*)

Now, we've made out the power of attorney and here she is herself to attest her signature.

SARNOFF

Oh, that will be quite needless.

VANCE

Well, I thought it might be best to have her come along. She was saying to me on the way over how pleasant it would be to have you associated with us in this little venture—a friend of Damon's and everything. Weren't you, Jessica, dear?

JESSICA
(*Nerving herself*)

Yes, Mr.—er—

VANCE
(*Hastily*)

Sarnoff. (*A gesture that bids her rise.*)

JESSICA
(*Smiling radiantly at Sarnoff*)

Sarnoff. It will be a great pleasure to have a man like you identified with the management. I hope we shall soon be better acquainted. (*She glances back at Vance as if for guidance*) You see, my husband is going on a trip. I shall be very lonely. Perhaps you will come in some evening for supper after the play.

SARNOFF

(*After watching her steadily through this speech, picks up the telephone*)

Would you be so good as to send a bellboy? Thank you. (*Turning to the others*) I am afraid you are going to think me a little rude. I have always found ladies at a business meeting a too great distraction. And on an occasion such as this, when Miss Wells herself is the very essence of our bargaining, surely you will understand my difficulty—I could not begin to do myself justice. (*He bows from the waist*) I am truly sorry.

VANCE

(*As* JESSICA *gives him a glance asking guidance*)

Not at all, not at all, Mr. Sarnoff. Don't say another word. No harm done, I'm sure.

SARNOFF

None, at all.

VANCE

(*He motions her to go—she rises*)

Anyhow, now that you're acquainted—

SARNOFF

One moment. I have asked for a page to escort Madame.

VANCE

Oh, thank you.

SARNOFF

(*After a slightly awkward pause*)

Well, Mr. Vance, so you, too, are going on a journey. Will you be away long?

VANCE

Well, I'm afraid so. It all depends. Of course that's the tragedy of this theatre business. Makes a wreck of home life. While Jessica is playing here, I have to be away, and like as not when I come back in town, my wife will be on tour.

SARNOFF

I see. It is very sad.

VANCE

Yes, during the greater part of our marriage, I have had to be away. Been out West for the last few years. California. (*There is a buzzer at the door.*)

SARNOFF

Will you be so good, Mr. Vance? My—er— (*He glances at his disabled arm.*)

VANCE
(*Going to the door*)

Certainly.

BELLBOY
(*Entering*)

Yes, sir?

SARNOFF
(*To the bellboy*)

Would you please escort this lady to a taxicab? (*With a bow to Jessica*) My apologies, Madame. We shall meet again.

JESSICA

Good-by, sir.

SARNOFF
(*to the bellboy*)

Young man, do you happen to have the time? My watch—

107

BELLBOY

(*Consulting his watch*)

Five past three, sir.

VANCE

(*Checking from his own watch*)

That's right.

SARNOFF

Thank you.

VANCE

(*As she starts towards the door*)

Wait for me at home, my dear. I shall be there soon.

JESSICA

Yes, Stanley. (*She goes out.*)

VANCE

(*Checking the bellboy with a touch on the arm and speaking
with a lowered voice*)

Tell the driver 205 East 48th St. (THE BELLBOY *goes out and
the door closes*) Well, I know you're a busy man, Mr. Sarnoff.
I suppose you want to get right down to business.

SARNOFF

Surely there is no hurry. You Americans! Mix yourself a
drink, Mr. Vance.

VANCE

Don't mind if I do. (*He goes towards the buffet*) These
conferences are thirsty work. How about you? (*He is busy
making a highball.*)

SARNOFF

If you please. I regret I cannot myself do the honors. A very
little soda, please, and not any ice.

VANCE

What's the matter with your arm? Hurt yourself?

SARNOFF

I was reckless. I went into your subway. They are dangerous
—those doors.

VANCE

I always take a taxi, myself. (*Delivering the drink*) Here you
are, sir.

SARNOFF

Thank you.

VANCE

(*Back mixing his own drink*)

You know, Sarnoff, there's something I'd rather like to say
before we talk turkey.

SARNOFF

Sir?

VANCE

It's this way. We're men of the world, Sarnoff. You and I.

SARNOFF

You do me too much honor.

VANCE

Not at all. Now, you don't have to tell me. Your interest in
this thing is not entirely in the play.

SARNOFF

Well?

VANCE

You know, when you said just now that Jessica would be the
essence of the discussion—I don't want you to think that went
over my head.

109

SARNOFF

Well?

VANCE

Well, before we discuss terms, I just want you to know it
will be all right with me. My wife and I—ah—

SARNOFF

Well?

VANCE

(*With a charming smile*)

I guess you know what I'm talking about. (*He takes a long
draught of his highball.* SARNOFF *does not drink. He keeps his
glass in his hand, and several times lifts it as if about to drink,
but each time says something which interrupts him.*)

SARNOFF

And now, Mr. Vance, as I understand the matter, you—you
control—fifty per cent of the play called "The Dark Tower."

VANCE

Right. (*He takes another drink. Pulls some papers from his
pocket*) I think I've brought along practically everything.

SARNOFF

Good! And of this share, you would consider selling all or
any part.

VANCE

Well—my going away—might as well sell it all.

SARNOFF

I assume, of course, that you include all of the various rights
—cinema, repertory, whatever there may be.

VANCE

Naturally. (*Finishes his drink.*)

110

SARNOFF

So now we come to the big question—what sum do you ask? Remember, I am not a rich man.

VANCE

(*His speech slowing ever so slightly*)

Well, Sarnoff, a play of this sort. Shown itself a success already. Ought to run thirty or forty weeks. California rights. Foreign. Lord knows what the picture will bring. Of course you want to get an outright sum. You can't trust those people on percentage. (*He blinks a little and mops his brow*) Close.

SARNOFF

There is no breeze to-day. Tell me, Mr. Vance, when you speak of California rights, is that apart from the cinema rights?

VANCE

Yes, indeed. That means regular stage production. (*He is growing groggy*) You see, there are all sorts of by-products. All in all, whole thing ought to make two or three hundred thousand dollars.

SARNOFF

As much as that?

VANCE

However—cash in hand—after all, you're taking a certain gamble—what do you say to fifty thousand dollars?

SARNOFF

Oh, come, come, Mr. Vance!

VANCE

Mind if I sit back a second? (*He puts his head back and closes his eyes for a second*) What did you say just now? (*He*

III

struggles to keep his wits) Yes, sir, and you're getting a wonderful woman, you old rooster!

SARNOFF

(*Speaking with sharp intensity*)

Vance! Vance! (VANCE *looks at him*) You do not recognize me, do you?

VANCE

Huh?

SARNOFF

You do not recognize me.

(VANCE *looks at him hypnotized.*)

We first met quite some years ago. I cannot begin to tell you how impatiently I have waited for this reunion.

VANCE

(*Struggling desperately to his feet, he retreats as far as possible, summoning his last strength to point at his emptied glass.*)

What was in that drink? (*As he staggers weakly back to his chair, SARNOFF begins methodically to draw on a pair of gray suede gloves he has taken from his pocket*) Who—who—who—

(VANCE *pitches over the arm of the chair and hangs there unconscious.* SARNOFF *springs to his feet—the limp and the bad arm forgotten. He pulls the helpless man back into the chair, bends over him, feels his heart. Satisfied that the man is out, he steps swiftly to the closet and throws the door open. Returning, he gets a purchase under* VANCE's *armpits and drags him over into the closet and deposits him on the floor. Next he gets the knife and returns to his task. You half see his figure as he bends over the prostrate figure. You next see him straighten up, take the towel from the shelf and emerge with the knife blade already concealed in the towel. He wipes the blade, and as he tosses the towel back into the closet, you see the blood stains on it. Knife in hand, he comes to his seat at the table and drops into it, breathless and shaken. Automatically his hand reaches out for his untouched highball. He remembers in time.)*

(After a pause, his gaze goes to the knife and he pulls himself together. Rising, he slips the knife into his pocket. There is a chair and rug to be straightened. Then, with his hands on the telephone, he pauses, summons his wits and lifts the receiver.)

SARNOFF

Would you be so good as to send a boy for some bags? Thank you. *(He hangs up the reeciver, and, with his gloved hands, swiftly wipes the entire telephone, wipes the surface of the desk, his glass, the desk lamp, wipes the polished surface of the chairs he has touched, the knob of the outer door. His last act is to shut the closet door, lock it, take out the key, wipe the knob, wipe the key and thrust it down into the upholstery of* VANCE's *chair. He is surveying his handiwork when there is a knock at the door. Slipping his arm back into the sling, and resuming the limp, he crosses and opens the door, being careful to take off the gloves only after he has done so.)*

THE BELLBOY

Yes, sir.

SARNOFF

There are two bags in the bedroom.

(The BOY *goes cheerfully to get them, while* SARNOFF *gathers up his stick and puts on his hat. He is waiting*

113

for help with his raincoat when the BELLBOY *emerges with the two bags, one of them initialed M. S.*)
Could I trouble you to help me?

THE BELLBOY

Yes, sir. (*He puts down the bags and helps* SARNOFF *on with his coat*) Going to leave us?

SARNOFF

I think I had better.

THE BELLBOY

(*A quick look around the room*)
Sure you haven't forgotten anything?

SARNOFF

I hope not.

THE BELLBOY

Nothing in the closet?

SARNOFF

No. Nothing at all. (*He goes out, followed by the* BELLBOY, *who first switches off the main lights and then, resting one bag on the floor, pulls the door shut behind him. Only the desk lamp remains lit, and it throws a simple beam on the closed door of the closet. For a moment you see the stage empty.*)

Curtain

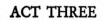

ACT THREE

ACT THREE

Scene I

The scene is once more the living-room of MISS TEMPLE'S *house.*

The time is nine o'clock of the following Thursday evening.

At the rise of the curtain, JESSICA, MISS TEMPLE *and* HATTIE *are on stage.* JESSICA *is at the piano, playing rather fitfully.* MISS TEMPLE *and* HATTIE *are busy with another session of their thirty-year cribbage contest. The cage with the mice stands on the floor at* HATTIE'S *feet.* DAMON *comes down the stairs, dressed in pajamas, bedroom slippers and bathrobe. He comes down at a jog-trot, humming to the music.*

DAMON
(In passing)
Hello, gamblers! (*He goes on out into the dining-room.*)

HATTIE
(Whose mind is really on the mice)
Eight.

MISS TEMPLE
Fifteen. (*She moves her peg two points; then, to recapture* HATTIE'S *attention, she repeats sternly*) Fifteen.

HATTIE
Twenty-four. (*She moves two points.*)

MISS TEMPLE

Thirty-one. (*Moving her peg.*)

HATTIE

(*First showing the card to the mice*)

Eight.

MISS TEMPLE

Fourteen. (*She waits in vain for the next play by* HATTIE, *who has become engrossed in the mice, poking her remaining card at them and clucking at them in an affectionate manner.* MISS TEMPLE *throws down her cards and rises in indignation*) Hattie, you are going to do one thing or the other. I will not play cribbage with an animal trainer. (*She begins sweeping the cards together as notice that the game is over. At the same time* JESSICA *stops playing with a crash and comes down stage.*)

JESSICA

(*Her voice high-pitched*)

Surely you two have nothing to wrangle about.

HATTIE

(*Engrossed in her pets*)

You know, I think Abercrombie has something the matter with his foot.

JESSICA

Maybe it's gout.

MISS TEMPLE

Hattie, I shall have to ask you to keep those insects in the kitchen.

HATTIE

I don't mind so long as you let me keep them. I think they're kinda cute. (*To the mice, in baby-talk*) Aren't you kinda cute?

DAMON
(Entering with a bottle of White Rock held by the neck in each hand and passing on upstairs)

Who won?

MISS TEMPLE
The *mice*.

HATTIE
I *was* winning.

DAMON
Tough luck, Hattie! Well, lucky in love— (*He goes.*)

JESSICA
(Mettlesome)

Of course you can keep them, Hattie. Why shouldn't you? I think they have great charm. Where did you say you got them?

HATTIE
(A little too quickly)

The iceman gave them to me.

JESSICA
Iceman? You'd better make up your mind, Hattie. Yesterday it was the milkman.

MISS TEMPLE
Of course it was the milkman. She doesn't know what she's talking about.

HATTIE
Yes, that's right—the milkman.

JESSICA
(After a pause)

Where *did* they come from, Aunt Martha? Did Stanley bring them?

MISS TEMPLE

(*Uneasily*)

Well—suppose he did?

(JESSICA *looks at them with a new interest. The two older women are helpless.*)

We—we didn't want to remind you.

JESSICA

Nothing reminds me. (*She walks to the steps*) And I can believe nothing you say. Let me know when the detective comes. (*She goes up the stairs.*)

MISS TEMPLE

(*Who has watched* JESSICA *out of sight, slowly shifts her gaze to the offender*)

Just no sense, that's the only trouble with you. No sense.

HATTIE

I got mixed up.

MISS TEMPLE

You've got no business having them around at all. You might have known something would happen.

HATTIE

(*Picking up the cage*)

Well, I'll keep them where she can't see them.

MISS TEMPLE

And another thing—see if you can hold your tongue a while. You talk about that man every chance you get. Nothing but the murder! The murder! You wallow in it.

HATTIE

Why not? I like to see people get their comeuppance. It's the most fun I've had since I left Albany.

MISS TEMPLE

Well, you don't have to tell everybody in New York about it.

HATTIE

I didn't.

MISS TEMPLE

You told all the reporters. Hanging out of the kitchen window. Giving interviews.

HATTIE

Well, he was a very nice young man. His name was Whittaker. He used to be married to an actress himself once. I forget her name.

MISS TEMPLE

What's that got to do with it?

HATTIE

Well, he wants me to write my own story for the paper and he's going to write it for me.

MISS TEMPLE

Don't you dare let him!

HATTIE

(*A little sulkily*)

Oh, all right. But that stenographer girl in the hotel wrote *her* story. "Patsy Dowling's Own Story." I read it. And I saw him *too*, didn't I? That Mr. Sarnoff. I opened the door for him. And if I hadn't opened the door for him—

MISS TEMPLE

(*Wearily*)

Yes, Hattie, you started the whole thing. Accessory before the fact.

HATTIE

Well, there's no use calling names. Anyway, I didn't go down and look at the body the way you did.

MISS TEMPLE

Some one had to identify him.

HATTIE

Mr. Damon was there.

MISS TEMPLE

Well, I wanted to make sure. And I made sure. (*An emphatic nod of the head*) If he comes back this time, he's a wizard.

HATTIE

(*Who has been exploring the evening paper, speaking sadly*) They've got it way on the inside now. Just a little bit of a piece.

MISS TEMPLE

You can't stay on the front page forever. It's been five days.

HATTIE

(*Reading*)

"POLICE MIZZLED BY WALDORF KILLER."

MISS TEMPLE

Mizzled?

HATTIE

That's what it says. M-I-S-L-E-D.

MISS TEMPLE

Oh!

HATTIE

It says they don't think Mr. Sarnoff really jumped off of that boat.

122

MISS TEMPLE

I told you you wallowed in it. You *like* to be reminded of him. (*She points to the cage*) Hanging on to those. You even wanted to keep all those pajamas he ordered.

HATTIE

They were silk.

MISS TEMPLE
(*Suddenly suspicious*)

You *didn't* keep them, did you?

HATTIE

No, I didn't. The Salvation Army came this morning and I gave them to him.

MISS TEMPLE
(*Relaxing*)

Hmm. I'd like to be there when they hand out silk pajamas to those Bowery bums. Monogrammed. (*The doorbell rings*) It's probably the doctor. I'll go. You take that menagerie out of here.

> (*As* HATTIE *catches up the newspaper, clipping, scissors and cage and starts for the dining-room,* MISS TEMPLE *goes to the hallway. Just before she reaches it, she calls over her shoulder to the disappearing* HATTIE.)

MISS TEMPLE

And you'd better get some drinks ready. They'll want them.
> (*There is the sound of the door opening.*)

Oh, it's you!

DAPHNE

Good evening!

MISS TEMPLE

Come in, won't you?

(*Enter* DAPHNE, *followed by* BARRY *and* MISS TEMPLE. *They are both in evening clothes and* BARRY *carries her cloak over his arm.*)

DAPHNE
We can't stay long. Is Damon here?

BARRY
We just popped in for a minute.

MISS TEMPLE
He's upstairs. (*She calls out*) Damon! (*Calling out again*) Damon!

DAMON
(*Heard off*)
Coming!

DAPHNE
What's the matter? Isn't he up yet?

BARRY
We don't want to bother him.

DAPHNE
Oh, yes, we do. (*Glancing around the room*) Say, this room's different. You've taken something out of here.

MISS TEMPLE
What do you mean?

DAPHNE
The last time I was in it, Stanley Vance was sitting right there. It's much better this way.

MISS TEMPLE
I'm glad you think so. We like it.

DAPHNE

(*Pointing to the Lionel Wells portrait*)

You ought to take that down and put up a picture of that man Sarnoff.

MISS TEMPLE

(*With a nod of assent*)

Yes, too bad we can't get one. He didn't even come around to be thanked.

DAPHNE

He certainly gave you people a lovely present.

MISS TEMPLE

Don't think we didn't appreciate it. Though personally I don't hold with accepting gifts from perfect strangers.

DAPHNE

Wish he'd come around to my house. I've got a few odd jobs he could have done.

BARRY

Tell me, Miss Temple. How's Miss Wells? She all right now?

MISS TEMPLE

She's coming along. She'll be fine in a day or two.

BARRY

Maybe I oughtn't to talk shop just yet, but we sort of wondered when she'd be ready to play again.

MISS TEMPLE

She'd be ready almost any time, but I don't suppose it would look very well. Opening so soon afterwards.

DAPHNE

I don't know why not. You could use the same flowers.

125

DAMON

(*Coming down the stairs*)

Well, I'll be damned! How long have you two been a team?

BARRY

Hello, Mr. Wells.

DAMON

(*Coming on down the steps*)

Jones & Martin, card tricks and sex appeal.

(HATTIE *enters with a tray containing decanters, White Rock, cracked ice and glasses, places it on the table and presently goes out again.*)

MISS TEMPLE

I'll tell Jessica you people are here. She may want to see you.

(MISS TEMPLE *goes up and out.*)

DAPHNE

(*As she starts to mix herself a drink*)

I see you're living at home again. Did you get put out of anywhere?

DAMON

No, darling. Sorry.

DAPHNE

Want a drink, dear?

BARRY

Yes, please. Small one.

DAMON

Dear, eh? So that's the way it stands.

DAPHNE

Yes, and what of it? And while I think of it, you put on a

pretty nasty act the last time I was here. What was the big idea—jumping down my throat that way?

DAMON

What? I haven't been near your throat.

DAPHNE

You know what I'm talking about. Right in this room last Saturday, when I said you went to Philadelphia.

DAMON

Oh, that.

DAPHNE

And when I started to say I'd seen you at the Waldorf— why, you pretty near knocked me down. Any one would have thought I was going to tell where you'd hidden the body. (*A new light dawns on her*) Say, what were you doing around there, anyhow? Calling on Mr. Sarnoff, by any chance?

DAMON

(*Delighted with her*)

So that's it, is it? I'm supposed to have hired Sarnoff.

DAPHNE

Well, I wouldn't put it past you.

DAMON

Hmm. I should have engaged him to mop up Horace here. Stealing my woman, you snake.

BARRY

We're just going to the Casino and dance.

DAMON

That's what *you* think.

127

DAPHNE

Say, here's what we came for. Do you know when you're going to do this play? Or if you're going to do it at all?

DAMON

Sure we're going to do it—when we get around to it.

DAPHNE

Well, I wish you'd tell me when.

BARRY

Honey, don't be impatient. The delay's been useful, hasn't it?

DAMON

Useful? How come?

BARRY

(*A little flustered*)

Well, it's given me a chance to rewrite a couple of scenes. I always wanted to rewrite a couple of scenes.

DAMON

(*A light dawning*)

I see. Not by any chance a couple of scenes in which Miss Daphne Martin appears?

BARRY

Well, in a way, yes.

DAMON

Don't tell me you've been cutting her part.

DAPHNE

(*As* BARRY *fumbles for words*)

Well, the new stuff is much better for the play.

DAMON

You must let me hear it before we open. Well, well, so you've

128

a new inspiration, eh, Barry? Tchekhov began that way. Yes. It killed him, but she's still got the part. Ah, my boy, treat her gently for my sake. (*He leads* DAPHNE *over and puts her hand in* BARRY's) Remember, she's just a shy and frightened child, a little old-fashioned flower, sweet as a violet, pure—in moderation. Take her, my boy, take her in your great rough arms— (*There is a ring at the doorbell*) and incidentally take her out of here, because I think this is a man I've got to talk to.

DAPHNE

Just a pal, aren't you?

DAMON

Don't mind me, Barry. I'm just a bitter old man. Tell you what. Weston's coming in later. Suppose you telephone me in the morning. I may have some news for you.

BARRY

All right. About eleven?

DAMON
(*To* BARRY)

O. K. Eleven.

CURTIS
(*At the door*)

Can I see Mr. Wells?

HATTIE

Come right in.
> (CURTIS *enters. He is a mild-mannered, middle-aged man, rather slow in his movements. He has his hat in his hands.*)

DAMON

Ah, there, Mr. Curtis. Come right in. Take a seat, won't you? These people are just going.

129

MISS TEMPLE

(*On the stairs*)

Who's that? Oh, good evening, Mr. Curtis.

CURTIS

Howdy, Miss Temple.

BARRY

Well, good night, then. I'll call you to-morrow. (*Goes into the hallway.*)

DAMON

Good night.

DAPHNE

(*To* DAMON, *with a wary eye on the hall*)

Listen—as soon as he's tucked in his crib I'll call you up. (*She goes.*)

DAMON

Little blossom.

(*The sound of the door closing.* HATTIE, *incidentally, has hung hopefully around since the entrance of* CURTIS.)

MISS TEMPLE

(*Who has brought down her knitting*)

Well, Inspector, you're quite a stranger around here. What have you found out?

CURTIS

(*As he starts to seat himself, gets out his notebook and spectacles*)

Oh, lots of things.

DAMON

For instance, he's discovered that a mystery woman named Hattie is lurking in this room. (*He shoos her towards the*

130

dining-room) If he wants to grill you, Hattie, we'll send right out for you.

(HATTIE *goes, heartbroken.*)

MISS TEMPLE

Anything to drink, Inspector?

CURTIS

No, thanks. I can't drink and work.

DAMON

I quit working.

CURTIS

Well, you people know what I'm here for to-night. It's about time I had my talk with Miss Wells.

MISS TEMPLE

She'll be right down, Inspector. If you wouldn't mind waiting a few minutes—the doctor wants to be here when you talk to her. You know, she's not very strong yet.

CURTIS

No change in her, I suppose? Still can't remember anything?

MISS TEMPLE

Not a thing. The doctor will tell you. You won't learn a thing from her.

CURTIS

Well, I suppose not. But I've got to try. My report goes in to-morrow morning. The chief would think it pretty funny if I hadn't even talked with her. The last person who saw him alive. I've got to tidy things up. You know, this is my last night on this case.

DAMON

Really? You can't consider it closed.

131

CURTIS

Well, these cases are never closed till we catch the murderer. But I'm going on my vacation to-morrow.

DAMON

That so? For long?

CURTIS

Two weeks. Going up to Vermont. My wife's sister's got a place up there. So we're getting out the old bus and driving up. Taking the boy along. The girl won't go.

MISS TEMPLE

My! We'll certainly miss you. I didn't know detectives went off on vacations. I mean when they had a case on.

DAMON

She wants you to be relentless and get your man.

CURTIS

(*Equably*)

Well, of course I'm as relentless as I can be. But I handle a lot of cases in a year's time and it's hard to be relentless about all of them. You see, we have about eight to ten new murders a week. Sometimes more.

MISS TEMPLE

Good gracious! Why don't we hear more about them?

CURTIS

Well, they're not all killed at the Waldorf, in the first place. And they're not all linked up with any one so well known.

MISS TEMPLE

(*Drawing her chair closer*)

Tell me, Inspector. What makes you think this Sarnoff didn't

really kill himself? The papers came out Monday and said he
jumped off the boat.

CURTIS

Well, maybe he did. But if I had to bet, I'd say he didn't.
Now what do we know he did do? We've got him leaving the
Waldorf in a taxi at— (*He consults his notes*) twenty-five minutes after three. We located that driver—Clifford Thackeray.
Now, when he left the hotel, he had two bags with him. The
bellboy carried them downstairs and the porter put them in the
cab for him. Now, Thackeray drives him to the Pennsylvania
Station—Pennsylvania side. He gets out and there we lose track
of him. All right. Next morning the Boston nightboat docks at
Boston and reports a missing passenger. In the stateroom is a
bag marked M. S., and the boat-steward remembers that a
foreign-looking gentleman, plainly our man, got on the boat
about an hour before she sailed—say four o'clock—locked himself in the stateroom and said he didn't want to be disturbed.

MISS TEMPLE

Looks to *me* as if he killed himself.

CURTIS

Maybe he just wanted you to think so. Maybe he left the boat
before it sailed. Because there was only one bag found in that
stateroom. If he killed himself, what became of the other one?
Did he throw it overboard?

MISS TEMPLE

Well, I never thought.

CURTIS

And on top of that, there's this. He'd just enjoyed a sweet
revenge, probably was feeling fine, no reason to think we were

going to catch him. Why should he kill himself? And then those letters—the stuff he dictated to the Dowling girl. She had something like seventeen letters in her notebook. Most of them about nothing at all. Of course we can't rely too much on those letters but if a man's going to kill himself, he doesn't sit down and write a lot of foolishness—to the Editor of the *Times* about the Aquarium, to the head of the Public Library, complaining about the lions— No. He didn't kill himself.

DAMON

Wrong mood, eh? Well, that applies if he knew he was going to commit a murder. But suppose it was a sudden flareup—burst of temper, a fight?

CURTIS

This was no flareup. Remember the doped whisky? You don't have knockout drops ready if you're not expecting company.

DAMON

So you're still looking for Sarnoff. What are your chances? Think you'll ever find him?

CURTIS

Oh, we may stumble upon him some day. Like as not when we're least expecting it. Tell you the truth, we don't much care in a case like this. As I size it up, with all due respect to you people, it's a case of one crook killing another. We never object to that. And when on top of that, they're not even New York crooks— (*He gives a dismissive wave of the hand*) —well!

DAMON

How do you know Sarnoff was a crook?

134

CURTIS

Oh, it all points that way. He seems to have come to town for the sole purpose of settling an old account with this man Vance. Probably followed him here, as a matter of fact. Now, who was Vance? Again offering my apologies, he seems to have been an out-and-out crook. Served a couple of jail sentences, used two or three different names—

DAMON

I'll admit Vance was a crook, but how do you know Sarnoff was?

CURTIS

Well, when one crook is done in, it's dollars to doughnuts another crook did it. Generally works out that way. But I've got better proof than that. This man Sarnoff was in that hotel room five days, Monday to Saturday. We've been over every inch of that suite and he never left a single print. Now, what does that mean? It means his finger prints were on file. He was not only a crook, but a known crook.

DAMON

Of course. I never thought of that.

MISS TEMPLE

Two or three different names, you said. His real name was Vance, wasn't it?

CURTIS

(*Flicking over his notebook*)

No, no. We've got him pretty completely documented. His real name was Marcus Blaine. Came of pretty good people in Fall River. Born there in 1887. Father was a manufacturer. Died early. His mother brought him up. Abroad, mostly. Florence. Rome. Had a house near Paris for five or six years. Place called—Noo-illy. The mother died in 1909. Left him a little money and he got rid of it in about a year. Got in some scrape with a woman down in Memphis, and the next time we pick up his trail he was calling himself Stanley Vance and was married to a woman named Applegate. That was in 1912, in Frederickton, Maryland. The following year, she committed suicide.

DAMON

The hell she did.

CURTIS

He spent the war in South America. God knows what he did down there. Came back to the States in 1923. Anyhow that's when we pick him up in Seattle. By that time he was Marcus Blaine again. He got five years out there for grand larceny. Swindled some old woman. Seems she signed a lot of papers when she was supposed to be hypnotized. Personally, I don't take much stock in that sort of thing, but that's what the district attorney claimed: hypnotized. Anyhow, the jury believed it. The rest I think you know. San Quentin, and all that. All in all, he seems to have been quite an operator. One thing I'd like to know, if you don't mind telling me, is how a woman like Miss Wells ever came to marry him? Where'd she meet him, anyhow?

MISS TEMPLE

She met him on a boat going to Europe. They got married in Paris before I'd ever seen him.

CURTIS

You women certainly marry strange men.

MISS TEMPLE

I don't.

136

DAMON

I suppose you haven't got hold of any of Sarnoff's past—where *he* came from?

CURTIS

No, he seems to have dropped right out of the blue. Of course, we probably know him well enough under some other name. Registered from Tulsa. We went through the motions of looking him up out there, but we weren't surprised when they said they'd never heard of him. If we could have found the taxi driver that brought him to the Waldorf, we might have got a line on where he came from. All we know is, he arrived there about ten o'clock Monday night—five days before the murder. We've talked to every one around the hotel who saw anything of him. Room-clerks, bellboys, stenographer—of course she saw the most of him. Saw a little too much of him, if you ask me. Seems to have been sort of attracted to him. I don't know what went on there.

DAMON

You don't say!

CURTIS

Let's see. Chambermaid, girl at the news-counter. She had to send out and get a Tulsa paper for him every day.

DAMON

That was rather a nice touch if he didn't come from Tulsa.

CURTIS

Head-porter. Guess that's about all. Never used the barber or the manicurist. (*Spotting a note in his book*) Oh, yes! We had the chambermaid identify the contents of that bag, but it didn't get us anywhere. There was some haberdashery—all of it new stuff that can be bought anywhere and didn't have any laundry marks. The toilet articles—another blind alley. Mono-grammed "M. S." but came from a shop in London that's been out of business since the War. (*With a snap of his fingers*) Gee, I almost forgot that. Eight dollars and fifty cents for cabling. Make it nine dollars. (*He takes out another notebook and notes the expense*) Now, then, he only put in two phone calls in the five days. Both of them, as you know, to this house. Now, your Miss— (*He consults notebook*) —Miss Dollop has testi-fied—

DAMON

Who?

MISS TEMPLE

He means Hattie. Hattie's last name is Dollop.

DAMON

It is? I never knew she had a last name.

CURTIS

Now, she tells us that both those times he asked for you, Mr. Wells. Still no idea why, I suppose?

DAMON

Not a glimmer.

CURTIS
(*Meditatively*)

I wonder if Vance— No ... I'd like to talk to that hired girl of yours again.

DAMON

Certainly. (*He walks towards the dining-room*) Miss Dollop! Miss Dollop, would you be so kind as to favor us with your presence?

HATTIE

Yes, sir.

138

DAMON

Miss Dollop is en route.

CURTIS

(*As* HATTIE *enters expectantly*)

You answered the door when this man Sarnoff came here last Saturday. And Mr. Vance was in this room at the time.

HATTIE

Yes, sir. And Mr. Weston.

CURTIS

Now, you said that Vance seemed pretty excited when he heard Sarnoff's voice. Came right out into the vestibule.

HATTIE

Yes, sir.

CURTIS

Well, aside from his excitement, did he say anything that made you think he had known him before?

HATTIE

(*Vaguely*)

Well, he seemed awful glad to see him.

CURTIS

(*To the others*)

You know, that puzzles me. (*To* HATTIE) Had you ever heard Vance mention Sarnoff at any time?

HATTIE

(*To every one's surprise*)

Yes, sir.

CURTIS

You did? Well, why didn't you tell me that before? What did he say?

HATTIE

Well, it was the day Mr. Sarnoff came here. Just before. He knew I'd taken the telephone message and he called me in and asked me if Mr. Sarnoff left any number, if I knew where he could reach him. But he didn't get anything out of me.

DAMON

(*Cruelly*)

Well, you didn't know anything, did you?

HATTIE

No, but if I had he wouldn't have got it.

(*The doorbell rings:* HATTIE *hesitates as if she'd rather be cross-questioned, but when the detective seems to have lost interest in her, she goes to the door.*)

CURTIS

You know, that's very interesting. You see what that proves?

MISS TEMPLE

What?

CURTIS

Why, it's as plain as the nose on your face. It answers one question for me. It proves that Vance knew Sarnoff under the name of Sarnoff.

DAMON

(*With admiring comprehension*)

Ah!

(*The* DOCTOR *enters. He is wearing a dinner-coat.*)

KENDALL

I'm later than I meant to be. Good evening!

CURTIS

Hello, doctor!

140

KENDALL

Inspector, how's your case coming? Getting anywhere?

CURTIS

Oh, we're moving, but sort of in a circle.

KENDALL

By the way, what did your analysis show on that whisky?

CURTIS

Chloral hydrate. Pretty strong stuff. Acts quickly.

KENDALL

Yes, and there's no tracing it. You can get it anywhere.

CURTIS

Now what about Miss Wells, Doctor?

KENDALL

No change at all. She's well, perfectly well. But there seems to be a complete block. You know she fainted when the police brought the news last Saturday. Next morning it slowly dawned on us that one entire week had been wiped off her mind. Dropped out of her life as if it had never been. She didn't remember a thing from the time Vance got here until the time he was killed. She thought her play had closed in Greenwich the night before.

MISS TEMPLE
(*Rises*)

I'll get her. (*She goes.*)

CURTIS

What did it? Shock?

KENDALL

Defense mechanism, I think they call it. It's just an inner

141

necessity for her to forget what had been an intolerable experience. Of course it's not a rare phenomenon. We doctors run into it often.

CURTIS

Yes—so do we detectives. How long's it going to last? Forever?

KENDALL

You never know. That's the reason I held you off a few days. I thought it might come back to her. But now I don't think so.

CURTIS

Well, looks as if my talk with her is going to be pretty dull. All questions and no answers. Still—

JESSICA

(*Entering with* MISS TEMPLE)

Well! This seems to be quite a full session.

MISS TEMPLE

My dear, this is Inspector Curtis.

JESSICA

So, I'm finally to face the law, am I?

KENDALL

Now, Jessica dear, Inspector Curtis—

JESSICA

Yes, I know. (*She turns to the rest with a sweep*) I wonder if you people would mind leaving me alone with the Inspector.

MISS TEMPLE

But, Jessica—

JESSICA

I know what I'm doing, Aunt Martha. I have a reason.

142

DAMON

(*As they all hesitate*)

Of course. Come on, everybody. (*He leads the way into the dining-room.*)

MISS TEMPLE

(*As* DAMON, *the* DOCTOR *and herself go out*)

Damon, I don't like this.

DAMON

What can you do?

JESSICA

(*As the doors close*)

Please sit down. (CURTIS, *eying her speculatively, approaches a chair, and waits for her to seat herself. She drops into a seat, and he, too, sits.* JESSICA'S *speech is tense, low, controlled, animate with purpose*) Now, I know that you'll tell me the truth. I can't get it from these people. I haven't even tried. They think they're being kind when they lie to me. They kill me with their kindness. What I need is to know!

CURTIS

(*Gently but watchfully*)

What do you want to know, Miss Wells?

JESSICA

I want to know just what I did last Saturday afternoon—as far as you can tell me.

CURTIS

When you left the house?

JESSICA

When I left the house.

143

CURTIS

You and your husband left here about ten minutes to three. You took a taxi to the Waldorf and you went up to Suite 1970, occupied by a man registered as Max Sarnoff. By the way, did you ever know Max Sarnoff?

JESSICA

I never heard of him in my life before. What next?

CURTIS

Well, you yourself—you couldn't have been in that room more than three or four minutes when Sarnoff phoned down for a bellboy and told him to take you to a taxi.

JESSICA

Sarnoff told him—not my husband?

CURTIS

No, Sarnoff.

JESSICA

That's the same bellboy who came here Monday and identified me?

CURTIS

That's right.

JESSICA

Then what?

CURTIS

Well, he took you down and put you in a taxi and you must have come straight home. Anyhow, you were back here by a quarter past three.

JESSICA

That's all? You don't know anything that hasn't been in the newspapers?

CURTIS

Nothing, Miss Wells.

JESSICA

When I left that hotel room, Stanley Vance was still alive?

CURTIS

According to the bellboy.

JESSICA

He couldn't be mistaken?

CURTIS

Don't see how.

JESSICA

He'd have no reason to lie.

CURTIS

None whatever.

JESSICA

You yourself have no doubt?

CURTIS

(*His manner thawing towards her progressively*)
None.

JESSICA

Then—there's no blood on my hands. *Possibly.*

CURTIS

Not possibly.

JESSICA

Thank God! (*She bursts into tears, and for a moment sobs with her face buried in her hands.*)

CURTIS

(*Approaching her awkwardly*)
There, there, my dear.

JESSICA
(*Through her subsiding emotion*)

I am so relieved, so terribly relieved. It's—it's been growing inside me like a nightmare, this fear. At first I didn't dare admit it to myself. Finally it got to a point where I had to know. You can't realize what it means to have been some one else for a whole week, not knowing what that some one else has done. Oh, thank God!

CURTIS
(*Pacing ruminatively*)

Funny. I wait all week to question you and it finishes up with you questioning me. Still I guess it works out about the same. Feeling better?

JESSICA
(*With an explosive gasp of relief*)

Ah! You can't imagine! (*She walks towards the dining-room and flings the doors open. Her voice is triumphant*) People! Come back! Inspector, I love you! (*Half singing, she goes to the piano and rattles off something gay and spirited. Meanwhile the* DOCTOR *and* MISS TEMPLE *have returned.*)

MISS TEMPLE

Well, so we're to be let out.

KENDALL

Sounds to me as if the patient were improving. Inspector, you should have been called in sooner.

CURTIS
(*Gathering up his notebook, pocketing his spectacles*)

Yes, if you've got any more worries, Doctor, just let me know. It seems I can do practically anything at all except solve this case.

DAMON
(*Entering from the dining-room, highball in hand*)
Well, have you people played your big scene?

CURTIS
(*Retrieving his hat, from the floor*)
All finished, and just going. I'll bid you people good-by.

KENDALL
Satisfied?

CURTIS
Quite.

KENDALL
Convinced?

CURTIS
Convinced.

KENDALL
Good.

CURTIS
(*With a worried look*)
But before I go, there's one more thing. Miss Wells—

JESSICA
(*Coming forward*)
Yes, Inspector.

CURTIS
There's one thing I forgot to ask you.

MISS TEMPLE
Oh, my God!

CURTIS
You see, I've got a daughter—she was nineteen in April.
Smart as anything. And she's written a play.

147

DAMON

(*From the couch*)

Ah! Hah!

JESSICA

(*To Damon*)

Well, why not?

CURTIS

Of course, I don't know whether it's any good or not.

DAMON

(*Sotto voce*)

I do.

JESSICA

Shut up, Damon. Inspector, I'd love to read it. I want to act in it. Tell your daughter to send it to me immediately. Have her bring it herself. What's her name?

CURTIS

Gladys. That'll be fine of you, Miss Wells. She'll be terribly excited. (*He backs towards the door*) Thanks a lot.

JESSICA

And I want you and Gladys to come to my first night. I'll let you know when it is.

CURTIS

Say, that'll be wonderful.

JESSICA

Good! Where shall I send the seats?

CURTIS

Just Police Headquarters. It's in the phone book. Good-by, everybody. (*Assorted good-bys from one and all.* CURTIS *departs.*)

148

KENDALL

(*With a sigh of relief*)

Well, exit the law.

DAMON

(*Recitation*)

"The law is the true embodiment of everything that's excellent."

MISS TEMPLE

Anybody want any more drinks? (*She gathers up the tray and carries it out into the dining-room.*)

KENDALL

Well, I must be going, too. (*He pats Jessica on the shoulder*) I fancy you won't be needing me any more.

JESSICA

Nonsense! I'll want you to hold my hand all during rehearsals.

DAMON

Say, it might save money if we put him in the play. (*To the doctor*) Can you act?

KENDALL

I'm afraid not.

DAMON

You're *in*.

JESSICA

Damon, when can we start rehearsing? What *has* become of Ben?

DAMON

Well, sis, we were just waiting for you.

JESSICA

I'm ready. I'd be ready to-morrow if you think it would look

149

all right. Suppose we open in about two weeks? What's the worst people could say?

DAMON

They could say it was lousy. (*The doorbell rings*) Well, now we can decide. Here's Ben.

KENDALL

I'll let him in. Good night, children.

    (*As he goes into the hallway,* HATTIE *appears in the dining-room doorway and retreats again.*)

JESSICA

Good night.

DAMON

So long, doc.

KENDALL

Hello, Weston! They're waiting for you.

WESTON

Good evening, Doctor. (WESTON *enters.*)

DAMON

Mr. Shubert!

JESSICA

Ben, I'm so glad. Where have you been? We thought you'd deserted us.

DAMON

Listen, Klaw & Erlanger, we two stage children are pining to act. Now, how about it?

WESTON

    (*His manner somber, embarrassed, unhappy*)

Well, you can go ahead. Just let my office know when you want to start. They'll attend to everything.

150

JESSICA

Your office?

DAMON

What's this—a new manner?

WESTON

That's what I came up here to tell you. Johnson knows all the ropes. You won't need me any more.

DAMON

What the hell's the matter with you?

JESSICA

Ben, what is it?

WESTON

There isn't anything the matter with me. I'm just going away, that's all.

DAMON

Going away? Where to?

WESTON

I'm going to Europe.

DAMON

To Europe? When?

WESTON

To-morrow night. *Ile de France.*

DAMON

Isn't this pretty sudden? In God's name, why?

JESSICA

(*Who has been watching* WESTON *intently*)
No, Damon. Let me. Ben, what's the matter?

WESTON

Nothing. Nothing. I'm just clearing out. I wish you the best of luck, Jessica. I hope you have a very great success. I'm sure you will have.

JESSICA

Ben, that's a farewell speech. (*She pauses for a denial that doesn't come*) I see ... Well, I don't suppose I can blame you. My life's been pretty messy, hasn't it? Perhaps you're wise to keep out of it. (*He is miserably silent*) (*She walks to the foot of the stairs*) Well, Ben—bon voyage. (*She goes up the stairs and out.*)

WESTON

Well—I must be on my way.

DAMON

Oh, no, Ben. Not yet awhile. I want to know what this is all about.

WESTON

She understands.

DAMON

I don't. God, Ben, will you stop playing "Hamlet"? What's on your mind?

WESTON

I don't want to talk about it.

DAMON

You've got to talk about it. Good God, haven't we been through enough in this house? I won't stand for it. I don't know what it's all about, but I will not have this whole thing kicked away for lack of a little plain speaking. Now out with it! Speak out and tell me what's the matter!

WESTON

For God's sake, Damon, don't make this any tougher for me!

DAMON

To hell with you and your feelings! I want to know what this is all about!

WESTON

(*With a struggle*)

All right. I'll tell you. Remember you asked for it. I was in this house last Saturday evening. I was here when the police came. I was with Jessica when she got the news.

DAMON

Well?

WESTON

You know she gave a terrible cry and dropped unconscious there on the floor?

DAMON

Well? What of it?

WESTON

Just this, Damon—it wasn't news to her.

DAMON

Not news to her? What do you mean?

WESTON

Since Vance was killed, she's been her old self again, hasn't she?

DAMON

Well?

WESTON

Damon, she was her old self again before that news ever came. I'd been here fifteen minutes. The change had already taken place. There was no mistaking it. She was as different as night from day. She knew it before the police ever told her.

DAMON

So that's it, huh? That's what you think.

WESTON

Now, don't get me wrong. I don't care if she killed him with her own hands. No one would blame her. I almost did it myself. But she put on an act. God, what an act she put on when they brought the news. Then I read she'd gone to the hotel that afternoon. Next I read she'd lost her memory. Well, maybe she has. Who can tell? After what I saw in this room, who can ever tell with her? She's too good an actress, Damon. I don't know where I am with her. I can see now I never would know. I couldn't stand it. It's best for me to clear out.

DAMON

You really think she had a hand in it, don't you?

WESTON
(*In misery*)

I'll never know. That's the trouble.

DAMON

I see. (*He paces the floor in thought*) There's only one person in the world— (*Another pause*) When are you going to sail? To-morrow night?

WESTON

Yes.

DAMON
(*Still thinking*)

Will you give me till sometime to-morrow to see what I can do about this?

154

WESTON

What is there you can do?

DAMON

I'm thinking mighty fast. I see only one way to do it. Will you give me till to-morrow afternoon?

WESTON

I don't understand this.

DAMON

(*Going to the drawer of the telephone table in the desk and poking there*)

Here's a key to this house. Say nothing to any one. Just come here to-morrow afternoon at—better make it six o'clock. Let yourself in and see what happens. Will you do that?

WESTON

I don't know what all this is. Must it be *here*?

DAMON

It must be here.

WESTON
(*Hesitating*)

I'm not crazy about it.

DAMON

Neither am I.

WESTON

You said six o'clock?

DAMON

Six o'clock on the dot.

WESTON
(*Pocketing the key with a sigh*)

I'll be here. Good night, Damon. (*He goes out and you hear the door close.*)

DAMON

(*Pacing thoughtfully, gives a quick glance up the stairs and goes to the telephone. He dials a number and waits a moment.*)

Dr. Kendall? Damon Wells. I want you to do something for me. To-morrow afternoon, just before six, I want you to get Jessica and Aunt Martha over to your house.

(*Pause.*)

That's all. I want you to get them over to your house. I don't care what pretext you use. You can invent anything you like. But get them over there and keep them there till I signal you.

(*Pause.*)

Well— (*With a glance around*)—I'll pull down the shade of the window nearest you. Have you got that straight? It's terribly important.

(*Pause.*)

A little before six.

(*Pause.*)

I'm counting on you. (*As he hangs up the curtain falls.*)

Curtain

ACT THREE

Scene II

The scene is the same. The time is the next afternoon a few minutes before five. As the curtain rises, HATTIE *enters from the dining-room. In her best clothes she is scarcely recognizable. She starts picking up a stray newspaper as* MISS TEMPLE *descends the stairs.*

MISS TEMPLE
(Who is slightly distrait)
What time is it, Hattie?

HATTIE
(Extracting her clipping)
Pretty near six. *(Her eye is ensnared by an ad)* What are pantasies, Miss Martha?

MISS TEMPLE
What?

HATTIE
They're having a sale of pantasies at Bonwit-Teller's—flesh-colored pantasies.

MISS TEMPLE
(Crossing to investigate)
What are you talking about, Hattie? *(She peers at the paper)* Yes, it does say Pantasies, doesn't it? Well, don't let me catch you buying any of them.

HATTIE

(*Regretfully*)

They look kind of cute on that girl.

MISS TEMPLE

You're built a little different, Hattie. Remember that bathing suit you bought when no one was looking last Summer? (*She sits down and starts to put on her gloves*) Pantasies!

HATTIE

Well, I might just look at them.

MISS TEMPLE

And you might just go on your way. Why aren't you out of here?

HATTIE

I'm going. But it's awfully funny, if you ask me.

MISS TEMPLE

What's awfully funny?

HATTIE

The whole thing. Mr. Damon sending me on an errand. He never sent me on an errand before. And you two going out at the same time.

MISS TEMPLE

Hattie, you see mysteries in everything these days.

HATTIE

All right, but what's he want to get us out of the house for? Empire Theatre, stage door. I've got to take a bundle to the stage door. (*With a descriptive gesture*) You ought to see it. I don't know *what's* in it.

MISS TEMPLE

You don't have to know what's in it.

158

HATTIE

You know what I think? I think he wants this house to himself. And I know why, too. He's got somebody up in that room.

MISS TEMPLE

Nonsense! What makes you think so?

HATTIE

Well, the door's locked, because I tried the handle and he just said "Go way."

MISS TEMPLE

Why shouldn't he?

HATTIE

That ain't all. I heard voices.

MISS TEMPLE

Don't be an old fool. He was probably rehearsing.

HATTIE

All right, but I've got it figured out. I'll bet he's got that Daphne Martin girl up there and he wants to get her out of the house without our seeing her.

MISS TEMPLE

Ridiculous! I never heard such stuff.

HATTIE

You mark my words, Miss Martha. And let me tell you this: When I get to the Sixth Avenue El, I'm going into the ladies' wash-room and open up that bundle. And if there's nothing in it but old newspapers, he's got that Martin girl up in his room.

MISS TEMPLE

Sherlock Holmes Dollop!

(HATTIE *goes, as* JESSICA *descends the stairs.*)

JESSICA

Wait a minute, Aunt Martha. I don't know why we've been sent for like this and I don't much care. But one thing I do know. I don't want you to say a word to Dr. Kendall about what's happened between Ben and me.

MISS TEMPLE

I don't know what's happened myself.

JESSICA

So much the better. Then say nothing about it. Don't even mention Ben's name.

MISS TEMPLE

The doctor's always known your troubles. He might be able to help.

JESSICA

I don't want to be helped. That's just it. I'm done with being helped. I've been helped so much, I'm helpless. Ever since I was a little girl. Pampered and taken care of and thought for.

MISS TEMPLE

But, Jessica, why shouldn't you have been taken care of? We loved you so. You were such a good child.

JESSICA

I know. Docile. Always did just what I was told. And what is the result? I haven't any spunk. I've no mind of my own. No wonder I was so easy for Stanley.

MISS TEMPLE
(*Deeply shocked*)

Jessica!

JESSICA

From now on, I'm going to be different. I won't have people

deciding things for me. I'm sick at heart. Yes, but I don't want my fever charted and my pulse taken. I don't want to be pawed over. I don't want to be discussed. I'm tired of being a clinical case.

MISS TEMPLE
(*Her voice breaking*)
Why, Jessica darling! I've only done always what I thought was— (*She dissolves in tears*) I hope you never live to have the one thing you've given your life to described as a failure. There's never been a time—

JESSICA
Oh, my dear, my dear, I didn't mean it that way. I wasn't criticizing you. But you mustn't discourage the first spark of independence I've ever shown. I'm just trying to get a little of my self-respect back.

MISS TEMPLE
(*With subsiding emotion*)
I know what I'm going to do. I'm not wanted around here any more. I'm going to take a little place somewhere and just sit out my days on a veranda. Perhaps I'll go up to Lake Mohonk.

JESSICA
(*Tender and amused*)
All right. And I'll come up and take the rocker next to yours. We'll both wear ice wool shawls and we'll sit and rock out our lives together.

MISS TEMPLE
Oh, dear, I can't go to the doctor's this way.

161

JESSICA

Of course you can. There's an idea. We'll make *you* th
patient.

MISS TEMPLE
(*Drying her eyes*)

What time is it?

JESSICA
(*With a glance at the clock*)

Oh, six almost.

MISS TEMPLE
(*Starting for the door*)

Good gracious! He told us four times to be there on the do

JESSICA
(*As they go out*)

Oh, we'll be in time. (*The door is heard closing. The stag
is bare for a moment. Enter* HATTIE *from the dining-room, he
walking costume completed by the addition of a hat and bo
She has the offending bundle under her left arm. She crosse
and goes out. Again the door is heard opening and closing
Again a bare stage.*)

(*The clock strikes six.*)

(*After a moment's pause,* MAX SARNOFF *enters on th
landing. He is dressed much as we saw him in his room
at the Waldorf. The limp, the cane, the black-silk slin
are as before. He comes slowly down the stairs, lookin
the room over. Once down, he completes his survey an
decides to close the doors into the dining-room. Next h
places two chairs half a dozen feet apart, facing eac
other. As if satisfied, he sits in the one facing the door
draws out a package of cigarettes, extracts one, an*

using only his left hand, lights it. He is smoking it thoughtfully, when the key is heard turning in the lock of the outer door. At that sound, he rises and stands expectant beside the chair. Enter WESTON.)

WESTON

(*Thunderstruck on the threshold*)

You're—you're Sarnoff! Well, I'll be God-damned!

SARNOFF

And you are Mr. Weston.

WESTON

(*Sparring for time*)

Yeah! Yeah! (*He glances up the stairs and back again*) Where's Damon Wells?

SARNOFF

He will be here soon. There is no cause for alarm. Please sit down. (WESTON *guardedly takes his seat.* SARNOFF *seats himself*) I am here, Mr. Weston, at the request of Damon Wells. He is an old friend of mine. I have known him all his life.

WESTON

Ah! Then you knew him before—I mean—was Damon in on this whole—

SARNOFF

I shall come to that. Now, Mr. Weston, I learn from Damon that you are troubled by doubts as to the complicity of his sister in the episode at the Waldorf.

WESTON

Not complicity exactly—her knowledge.

SARNOFF

Her *guilty* knowledge.

WESTON

(*Half assenting*)

Well—

SARNOFF

At least you believe that she already knew about the killing when the news came.

WESTON

Well—

SARNOFF

I have come here this afternoon with great difficulty, Mr. Weston, and at no little peril to my friend Damon, solely to convince you that you are mistaken. Until that closet was opened at 7:30 o'clock that evening, I was the only living person who knew what was in it. If the tidings had already reached her, it was by some method of communication which science does not yet understand. Maybe when that black heart stopped beating, there was effected in her some form of instantaneous release. "There are stranger things in Heaven and earth, Mr. Weston, than are dreamed of in your philosophy."

WESTON

(*Rising and pacing*)

God, I'm a fool. I guess I should have had more faith. Where is Jessica? Do you know?

SARNOFF

I believe she has gone out. I am not supposed to see her. I am only waiting for our friend Damon to return.

WESTON

(*Abstractedly*)

Oh, I see.

164

SARNOFF

(*Rising*)

He is a great fellow, Damon, and a great actor. He tells me, Mr. Weston, that you consider him the greatest actor in the world to-day.

WESTON

(*His thoughts elsewhere*)

Yes, he's pretty good.

DAMON

(*In his own voice*)

Pretty good, Hell! He's perfect!

WESTON

(*Staggered*)

What?

DAMON

(*Stretching himself luxuriously and abandoning all the* SARNOFF *impersonation*)

Hello, Ben, how's tricks! What are your plans for the season, Mr. Weston?

WESTON

Holy God! (*He gesticulates helplessly*) Holy God!

DAMON

Is that all you've got to say? No tributes of any kind?

WESTON

You! Of course, of course! My God, I was blind! Who else could it have been?

DAMON

(*Gratified*)

Thank you.

165

WESTON

Let me piece this thing together. Why, you even fooled me. I saw you in this room that day.

DAMON

That's nothing. I fooled you again just now. You know, years from now, when they discuss Irving, Booth, Mansfield—only you and I will know that those boys were merely adequate.

WESTON

I'll be damned.

DAMON

You don't blame me, do you, Ben?

WESTON

Blame you? Why, I was going to do it myself. I was *doing* it myself when that— Say, that was *you* came in. When did you start on all this? When did you get the idea?

> (*He has been slowly peeling off all the trappings of* SARNOFF, *the false teeth, the wedges in the nostrils, the high, confining collar, the coat, the attached shirt-sleeves fastened into the coat, even the false paunch. By the time he retreats, he is* DAMON *in extreme negligee, with nothing on above the waist except his undershirt.*)

DAMON

Well, I knew that first night that the thing had to be done. The only question was how. You want to know what started me off! There was an ad in the paper next day—Sunday—Pennsylvania railroad, auction of unclaimed baggage, Broad Street Station, Philadelphia. So I went over there and bid in a half a dozen bags at a total cost of seven dollars. One of them was just what I wanted—a man's suitcase with stuff in it about my size.

WESTON

But the initials on it. "M. S." That was pretty lucky.

DAMON

Ben, dear, *think*. If the initials had been L. B., the police would now be looking for a Mr. Lemuel Bumblebee.

WESTON

Not very bright, am I? But what did you do then? Where did you make the change?

DAMON

In a hotel over there. Went right out and bought fixings. Incidentally, some friend of Daphne's saw me there and Daphne waltzed in here one day and pretty near spilled the beans right in front of Vance. God, did I throw her out? I scared her right into bed with Barry.

WESTON

It must have taken a lot of nerve to walk right in here.

DAMON

Well, I worked up to it. Five days' rehearsal. That's all I ever need. Of course I wrote my own part. I did it gradually. I tried myself out on the mirror. Limped around the lobby. Talked to the bellboys. Made friends at the news counter.

WESTON

And that stenographer.

DAMON

Well, that's where I really worked on the accent. I dictated some very choice letters. Didn't mail 'em, of course. Then I decided to try myself out on the family.

WESTON

That was a risky moment.

167

DAMON

What's the worst that could have happened? I might have been recognized. Well, there's no law against wearing false teeth. No, the bad moment was in the hotel. When that door opened and Jessica walked in. That was something I hadn't counted on. You should have seen me keeping my hands out of sight. I still think, if she'd been herself, she'd have known me.

WESTON
(*Rises*)

What a boy!

DAMON

It wasn't perfect. I bungled that suicide off the boat. They never really believed that. Only made them suspicious. Oh, well, I'll do a better job next time. (*He crosses over to the window*) Shall we join the ladies? (*He pulls down the shade.*)

WESTON

Tell me, how does it feel to be a murderer?

DAMON

Feels fine.

WESTON

Ten commandments don't bother you? "Thou shalt not kill?"

DAMON

How about "Thou shalt not commit adultery?" That ever bother you?

WESTON

Well, that's so.

DAMON
(*Starting up the stairs*)

Say, I've got to get out of here.

168

WESTON

Well, Damon, it was great of you to do this, this afternoon.
With all the risk it meant. I thank you from the bottom of my
heart.

DAMON

Don't be silly. I was itching to tell you. Do you think I
wanted to give a performance like this and not get any notices?
(*There is the sound of the front door closing.* DAMON
vanishes up the stairs.)
(*Enter* JESSICA.)

JESSICA
(*In surprise*)

Ben!

WESTON

Jessica, that lapse of memory of yours—would you extend it
to include the events of last night?

JESSICA
(*After a long pause*)

When do we open?

WESTON

Whenever you say.

JESSICA
(*With mingled fondness and relief*)

Ben! Ben! Ben! (*Severely*) What about Europe?

WESTON

Well, what about it? You say.

JESSICA

After the play closes. We'll both go. (*He lifts her hand to his
lips and kisses it.*)
(*Enter* MISS TEMPLE.)

169

WESTON

I'm very ashamed.

JESSICA

Oh, my dear, nothing ever happened until a minute ago.

WESTON

It's the beginning of the world, isn't it?

JESSICA

The beginning of the world.

MISS TEMPLE

I told you the doctor might help.

DAMON

(*Appearing on the stairs in his bathrobe, while he scrubs his face with a towel*)

What's going on here? Can't a person sleep? (*With great surprise*) Hello, Ben!

WESTON

(*Also loyally surprised*)

Hello, Damon!

MISS TEMPLE

Oh, you're up, are you? Can't seem to get you out of the house these days. Where were you last week when we needed you?

DAMON

Auntie, you'd be surprised.

(JESSICA *is at the piano. There is a burst of gay music as—*

The curtain falls